D0686776

SOVIET
COSTUME
AND
TEXTILES
1917-1945

SOVIET COSTUME AND TEXTILES
1917-1945

TATIANA STRIZHENOVA

Flammarion

RO1637910581
sscra

HOUSTON PUBLIC LIBRARY

This is the last book of Tatiana Strizhenova, a well-known Soviet art historian, who finished this volume shortly before her death. Her text is an invaluable contribution to the history of the Soviet Union, and one of the first studies ever undertaken on Soviet clothing design.

Translated from the Russian by Era Mozolkova
Picture Research by Elena Bespalova and Irena Korzhevskaya
Captions by Elena Bespalova
Designed by Yulia Likhova

ISBN 2-08013-515-5
Copyright © 1991 Avant-Garde, Moscow, Paris, Verona
All rights reserved. No parts of the contents of this book may be
reproduced without the written permission of the publisher.

Printed and bound in Italy

CONTENTS

INTRODUCTION

The Soviet art of clothing and fabric design dates from the October Revolution of 1917, and was considered one of the first achievements of the Soviet state. For such a complex domain of creative activity, the period of seventy-odd years constitutes, historically, a very brief span of time. During its short history the art of Soviet costume has traveled an interesting and unique path: the 1917 Revolution provided a new social foundation for the creation of clothing for the working masses by abolishing class privilege and discrimination. Thus the idea of designing mass clothes first arose.

The post-revolutionary decade witnessed the most brilliant changes in the history of Soviet clothing design. This is when outstanding Soviet garment designers started their careers, approaching their work as a sphere of real creativity, as a fine art. It was in those years that the principles of the new Soviet costume were formed and the projects for mass clothing evolved. Young designers, with Nadezhda Lamanova at their head, began designing clothes for ordinary men and women, taking into consideration the demands of their everyday working and living conditions. The formula "for whom the costume is created, from which fabric, and for what purpose" became the designers' motto of creativity for the entire decade.

In the 1930s, steps were taken to create a base for industrial production of mass clothing. The opening of the Moscow House of Clothing Design marked the beginning of a creative process of working out clothing designs that could be mass-produced at numerous garment factories. The intense debates that this triggered on the development of Soviet costume and textile serve to this day as an example of impressive, well-grounded, and principled criticism.

Since the subject of this book, Soviet fashion from 1917 to 1945, had never been thoroughly researched, the author often had to "plough up virgin soil," especially when working on the first edition.[1] After studying the subject for many years through state archives, museum resources and private collections, and gathering information and recollections from clothing artists of the older generation, as well as their relatives and friends, the author has been able to share a wealth of important documents and materials telling the story of the history of Soviet clothing design.

The study of the material was sometimes difficult because many of the garments have disappeared, and the author had to rely on archival photographs and sketches, and illustrations in books and periodicals. Nevertheless, the available information made it possible to trace the development of this decorative and applied art. Most of the materials used are included in the text of the present publication.

The scope of research was intentionally limited to the work of the Moscow designers — in those years the most important events in this field were taking place in Moscow; there the main garment institutions were created, the efforts of the first artists of the new Soviet costume took shape, and most of the archival materials were concentrated.

1.
The present edition is a new and much larger version of the author's book *Iz istorii sovetskogo kostiuma*, or *From the History of Soviet Costume* (Moscow, 1972), and its editions in Italy (1978) and in the USA (1986).

The Early History of Soviet Clothing Design

To understand the immensity of the task facing the young Soviet state in the field of clothes manufacture, it is necessary to understand what the garment industry in Russia was like by the time of the Revolution of 1917. It was one of the most backward branches of the economy in prerevolutionary Russia. The proportion of clothing that was industrially produced by 1917 did not exceed 3 percent.

Clothes were made primarily in small artisanal workshops that closely resembled medieval feudal manufactories. There was little access to raw materials or technology. The few garment-producing enterprises that did exist in prerevolutionary Russia were in the bigger cities: St.Petersburg, Moscow, Kharkov, Odessa, Kazan, and Nizhni Novgorod. Their owners included the well-known foreign and Russian firms Mandel, Rosenzweig, Tiel, and the Petukhov Brothers.

1

Clothes of the various estates of Russia — workers, petty bourgeois, officials, clergy — and the students' uniform at the end of the past century. Procession at Nizhni Novgorod on the occasion of the 100th birthday of Alexandr Pushkin in 1899.

2

Cavalrymen of Budenny's army near Perekop in 1920. The Red Army uniform was produced in 1919, but was obviously in short supply. The soldiers of Budenny's legendary division wore totally inappropriate clothes: coats and shirts, hats and caps, puttees and bast shoes. The helmets dubbed *budenovka* had not yet appeared.

1

2

Besides the individual enterprises, a cottage industry system was widespread in pre-1917 Russia that prospered especially during the "seasons," i.e., from March to July and from September to December. The rest of the year most of the craftsmen were unemployed. Seventy percent of them were women and children, since their work was the cheapest. They brought home the pre-cut pieces of clothing, and sewed them together with the traditional tailor's instruments: the needle, thimble, and smoothing-iron heated with charcoal. Each craftsman worked on an article of clothing from beginning to end.

Entire sections of cities that had garment-producing firms were occupied with tailoring. Contact between firms and craftsmen was maintained through middlemen, who covered all the expenses of the cottage industry, but also made huge profits from it. This deeply-rooted system hampered the development of capitalist production, and the garment-producing centers were fragmented and disorganized.

Mechanization was limited to the sewing machines that were sold in Russia by foreign firms, the best known of which was Singer. Little if any aesthetic appeal was evident in the clothes made in these primitive stages of machine production—tailors and dressmakers seemed to forgo creativity under this system.

The bulk of the machine-made clothes produced by the firms were ordered by the military establishment. A small percentage were garments for the Russian high society. Usually, luxurious, fashionable attire was brought from Paris or other European cities. Nevertheless, there were also Russian artist-designers, working in famous firms such as Madame Olga,

3

Registration of delegates of the Fifth All-Russian Congress of Soviets in 1918. The congress, which opened in July, abounded in dramatic events. It had among its delegates two hostile parties, those of the Bolsheviks and the Socialist Revolutionaries. The work of the Congress was interrupted for the suppression of the Socialist Revolutionaries' armed revolt. As their clothes show, both the former and the latter belonged to the same social groups.

Ivanova, and Lamanova, which served the Russian aristocracy. The best known of these designers today is Nadezhda Lamanova, mostly by her activities in the postrevolutionary period. Characterized by superb execution, refinement, and exquisite taste, the apparel of the courtiers and the Russian aristocracy could be masterpieces of tailoring, in no way inferior to foreign samples. In its cheaper variant, the fashion of the upper circles "trickled down" to the wardrobes of the middle and lower classes, acquiring its own details and decorations, adapting itself to the peculiarities of the wearer's social status, his tastes and his means.

As early as the 1890s, changes were occurring in men's costumes; and in the 1910s, women's clothing changed dramatically. Economic and social transformations were advancing the democratization of society. An increasing role was being played by the proletariat; the position of women evolved. This led to new types of clothing that were functional, practical, and suited to the living and working conditions of ordinary people: men wore worker's overalls, women wore blouses and long skirts and gradually abandoned the corset. By the beginning of the First World War, the prototype of today's familiar male suit appeared. This developed largely under the influence of sports and the growing role of mechanization, including the increasing popularity and availability of the bicycle.

The Russian costume, despite its frequent borrowings from the West, had quite a few original features. This attire was not being dictated by official fashion but was taking shape in the streets. Urban clothes became increasingly simple and comfortable, and their development was

4
The opening of the Fifth All-Russian Congress of Soviets in 1918. The Congress was held at the Bolshoi Theater in Moscow. The delegates sat on the parapet and on the steps between the columns, and many women were clothed in elegant white romantic dresses and beautiful shoes. Women who were involved in the political struggle before the revolution most often belonged to "respectable families," the educated and wealthy stratum of society. Much later they were replaced by the proletarians in red kerchiefs.

5

Students of the general compulsory education schools of the 1920s dressed in whatever they could find: Russian shirts, shabby coats, cloth caps, and *budenovkas*. Elderly and young workers and Red Army men received primary education at these schools.

6

Frame from the film *October* (1927): German and Russian soldiers fraternizing in 1917. The Russian soldier, in his uniform of the Russian tsarist army, is in the center.

7, 8

Frames from the film *Lenin in October* (1937). Political leaders of the revolution, mostly intellectuals, are dressed in well-made suits of quality wool. Revolutionary sailors address inflammatory speeches to the Petrograd inhabitants in October 1917.

5
6

8

7

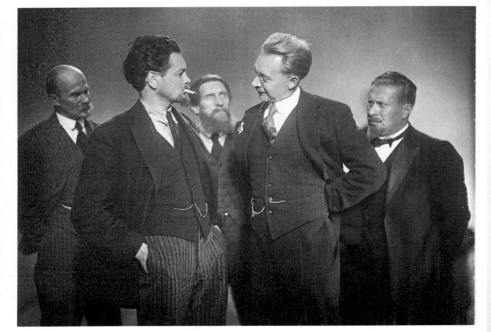

influenced by factors as diverse as social progress, current literary heros, and traditional Russian costume. Thus loose Tolstoy-style linen shirts became fashionable among the Russian intelligentsia in imitation of Leo Tolstoy or, to be more precise, as a token of solidarity with his ideological principles. Severe dark dresses with white collars were favored by female students and teachers, and capes and wide-brimmed hats were popular among male students. The Russian workers looked quite distinctive in the new proletarian garb of black sateen Russian shirts with collars that fastened on the side, coats, trousers tucked into boots, and peaked caps.

An interesting "style" was developed by the merchant class. It combined the forms of the peasant costume—*podiovkas*, men's long tight-fitting coats, and caftans—with the proletarian boots, peaked caps, and Russian shirts. Their clothes reflected the singularity of the Russian merchants' socio-political role.

In the countryside clothes retained their patriarchal features longer, owing to the more stable rural society. With the growth of industrial production, however, factory-made textiles began to oust the homespun in the countryside as well, and the men from the country who were hired in factories acquired a liking for the "town style," and spread it throughout the rural areas. The countryside thus began to absorb new forms of outer garments: short coats, peaked caps, Russian shirts made of factory-produced textiles, waistcoats, and urban *podiovkas*. Women increasingly wore one-piece dresses and skirts with blouses. Preference was given to the bright-colored, gay floral patterns of the Ivanovo and Moscow textile mills. Of course, these new styles were worn only on Sundays and holidays.

In 1914 many of the workshops were expanded due to large orders for the army; still, the general situation in textiles remained unsatisfactory. By the time of the October Revolution three years later, Russia still had an enormous network of handicraft workshops with an extremely low level of production. Civilian clothes remained at a primitive standard.

The October Revolution and the New Art

The October 1917 Revolution drew a dividing line between the old and the new art. The avant-garde called for a radical transformation of pre-revolutionary art and a renovation of its precepts. Art was to penetrate all sections of society and become accessible to all. The Soviet people's commissariats pursued an innovative program, fusing the notions of "revolution" and "art," while the bourgeois past was identified with the elitism and selectivism of prerevolutionary art. In this exhilirating period the first propagandists made passionate appeals for a democratic art. "Art into the Street! — this is the slogan of contemporary stage designers, actors, musicians, and architects. Let creative efforts now be made on a grandiose scale, not for a select few but for all, not for one's private apartment but for the 'occasional passer-by,' not to embellish one's home but to make the city beautiful."[2]

For the builders of the new society, the early 1920s were a time of daring efforts to transform art; a time of bold experimentation, imagination, and enthusiasm. Lenin's slogan "Art Belongs to the People" and his massive propaganda campaign formed the foundation on which the new future was built. A wide-ranging "Plan for Monumental Propaganda" was

2.
V. Kerzhentsev, "Iskusstvona ulitsu" in *Tvorchestvo*, 1918, no. 3, p. 12.

9
S. Gerasimov. *The Owner of the Land*, sketch for the town council building in Moscow, 1918. The revolution provided the peasants with land, and this was depicted in the immense panels decorating the cities on the first anniversary of the October Revolution.

10
I. Punin. Sketch for the decoration of *Liteiny prospekt* in Petrograd in 1918. The stratosphere balloon with the red banner — the symbol of a leap into the future — soars high above the crowd.

10

launched to design and set up monuments to revolutionaries and progressives in Russia and Europe.

New journals and newspapers were established as forums for discussion on the new culture. Appeals were voiced for a new way of life and a new kind of artistic education for the working classes that would make them capable not only of appreciating and analyzing culture, but also of creating it.

The revolutionary enthusiasm of the progressive artistic intelligentsia and their faith in the reshaping of culture were astonishing in view of the country's situation in the early 1920s. The builders of the new society had to work under conditions of grave economic dislocation, severe hunger, and even civil war. Many industrial enterprises stood idle because of the shortage of raw materials, fuel, and manpower.

A special commission of the All-Russian Council of National Economy, headed by V. Nogin, inspected the condition of the textile mills in Central Russia in 1919. This is what the Council wrote in its account of the country's biggest mill, owned by Emil Zindel: "Since 20 March of this year, the mill, owing to the absence of fuel, has completely shut down. Transportation difficulties have worsened because the barges that were to bring firewood received, due to Kolchak's offensive, a different assignment."[3]

3.
TsGANKh, f. 3338, op. 5, d. 12. Dokladnaya zapiska po obsledovaniu fabriki, "Emil Zindel," 12 maia 1919.

The volume of textile and garment production sharply declined. Textile goods shortages were extremely acute and lasted until the 1930s, reducing the availability and quality of clothes. Nevertheless, despite the tremendous difficulties, when matters of life or death of the new state were being decided, people redoubled their efforts. Artists focused their attention on the design and production of everyday items: furniture, tableware, kitchen utensils, and clothes. These manufactured goods were to reflect new ideas in culture, educate the mass consumer and form his

11
A column of pupils from one of the Moscow schools during the May Day demonstration in 1919 carrying a slogan calling for harmony and love, in a country torn by fratricidal civil war.

12
Poster by an anonymous artist of 1920 shows the worker of Soviet Russia raising the *Red Banner of World Revolution*.

11

12

13
V. Kozlinski. *The Worker*, sketch
for the decoration of Leningrad.
1920s.

14
Members of the Moscow *Proletkult*
(Proletarian Culture organization)
taking part in the demonstration
in Moscow, 1918, to observe the
anniversary of the October
Revolution.

13

14

taste. The term "industrial art" or *proziskusstvo*, was used to describe the new form these commonplace objects would take. There existed a deep conviction that people must give up old standards to shape a new society whose members were all created equal.

Archival documents and journal and newspaper articles of 1917-1920 abound in appeals to remodel daily life. A book of collected articles entitled *Iskusstvo v proizvodstve* (Art in Industry) was published in 1921. In its preface we read: "The problem of art in industry appears to us, in the light of the new culture, as one of the main preoccupations of emancipated labor. Having escaped from the philistine's apartment, where it was 'applied' by the old artistic culture, industrial art is taking root at the very heart of the new industrial forms and the creative process."[4]

The program of aesthetics that was taking root in industry was formulated with surprising precision, and its revolutionary significance was

4.
Iskusstvo v proizvodstve.
Moscow, Proletkult, 1921, p. 3.

made quite clear to the cultural workers of that time. Eager voices were raised in the defense of the tasks of industrial art and the "objective environment." Even critics who have left no noticeable trace in the history and theory of Soviet art offered a clear-cut platform. One of them, who signed his article with the assumed name of "Leonardo," said this about the demands of the revolutionary epoch: "Every executor, every craftsman must live up to the present-day artistic requirements. Every working man must understand what style means and be aware of the importance of the harmony of the environment, in which each object constitutes one of the colorful elements making up a beautiful artistic whole. The worker must not only understand what he makes, and for what purpose, but he must learn to create the entire object in its final form and in its connection and harmony with the whole."[5]

5.
Leonardo, "Iskusstvo i remeslo" in *Iskusstvo*, 1918, no. 6 (10), p. 6.

The slogan "Art for Industry" guided the creative work of a team of outstanding artists during the first five years of the 1920s: Nadezhda Lamanova, Liubov Popova, Varvara Stepanova, Alexandr Rodchenko, Alexandra Exter and others.

15
B. Kustodiev. *The Bolshevik*. 1920. The enormous figure of a Bolshevik, out of all proportion to the others, symbolizes the revolutionary epoch.

15

16

D. Moor. *First of May, All-Russian voluntary work day!* poster. 1920.

17

An amateur performance. *Red Army Review.* 1920s.

Stereotypes and the New Symbolism

It was almost universally agreed that the revolutionary epoch demanded new forms of mass clothing. The task was delegated to professional artists who could understand the laws of dress design. Meanwhile life changed rapidly in the young Soviet republic. Many artists occupied themselves, first of all, with the decorative work required for the celebration of the first revolutionary holidays, May Day and 7 November 1918.

In the decorative panels and placards produced for the festivities, many artists remained captive to the tenets of romanticism, depicting the revolutionary heroes wearing stereotypically classical, even sumptuous, clothes. The allegorical figures of Liberty in a white tunic, carrying a torch and riding in a chariot, and of the trumpeting Glory in flowing garments, personified the heroic and romantic spirit of the Revolution. This interpretation clearly had the protagonists of the bourgeois revolutions and the French Revolution as its source. Another representative of the holiday decorations was a muscular, half-naked worker with the tools of his trade: hammer, anvil, and wheelbarrow; a transformation of a generalized and abstract symbol into a brave Russian Hercules.

The principles of decoration employed in Petrograd (formerly St. Petersburg) for the first anniversary of the October Revolution were set forth in the report of M. Andreieva, chairwoman of the Central Bureau for the Organization of Celebrations, presented at the meeting of the Petrograd Soviet of Working People's Deputies on 24 September 1918: ''Torrents of our own and other people's blood are still being shed in the world; therefore the holiday, as we see it, should have a serious and sober nature. For there is still the proletariat, and there is still capital. The holiday should be clad, in our opinion, in red. Red is its color because it represents the triumph of our Socialist Red Banner, which has been persecuted for so long, and which today is in our hands and so proudly, so brightly, so joyfully flying over our heads.''[6]

17

6.
GAMO, f. 66, op. 3, d. 301, l. 159.

18

18
V. Lebedev. *Red Army and Navy defend the frontiers of Russia.* 1921.

19
V. Lebedev. *Worker at the Anvil.* 1920-1921.

20
A. Samokhvalov. *Long Live Komsomol!* poster. 1924.

19

ДА ЗДРАВСТВУЕТ КОМСОМОЛ

НА СМЕНУ СТАРШИМ

ИДЕТ МОЛОДАЯ РАТЬ

К СЕДЬМОЙ ГОДОВЩИНЕ ОКТЯБРЬСКОЙ РЕВОЛЮЦИИ

№87. ОРУЖИЕМ МЫ ДОБИЛИ ВРАГА
ТРУДОМ МЫ ДОБУДЕМ ХЛЕБ
ВСЕ ЗА РАБОТУ, ТОВАРИЩИ!

21

Photo of uniformed children, 1925.
The politicized organization for
children created in 1922 was
named Young Pioneers. The
Young Pioneers' uniform,
produced in 1924-1925, consisted
of skirts for girls, shorts for boys,
identical shirts for both, and red
neckerchiefs.

22

N. Kogout. *We have defeated the
enemy with weapons, we shall
make our daily bread with work...*,
poster. 1920.

23

May Day demonstration of 1925.

The importance of red in the holiday decorations was confirmed by the artists, who made extravagant use of it as the main color of banners, flags, stands, processions, and posters. Scarlet became the holidays' dominating semantic and decorative element, imparting both a solemn and an exalted character. It was from this first anniversary of the October Revolution that red began to attain its special, even exclusive, significance. The Red Banner and the Red Star were the emblems of the State of workers and peasants; the military began to be called the Red Army. Red was extensively used in clothes as well, and red triangular headscarves were extremely popular with socially active women.

24
Red Army men in greatcoats and
budenovkas. 1925.

25
Sketches of the Red Army
uniform: summer and winter
helmets, greatcoat, and soldier's
blouse. 1919.

The Red Army Uniform

The first example of the new Soviet garment was the Red Army uniform. Its emergence before other types of costume was dictated by a vital need: in the early months after the revolution, the Workers' and Peasants' Red Army still used the old uniform, but it was obvious that a new outfit was needed to symbolize a break with the past.

In April 1918, a temporary commission was set up to produce a new uniform, and a contest for the best design was announced. The terms of the contest did not specify details, but said only that the clothes must be comfortable, light, and democratically eliminate differences between ranks. Although the contestants were asked to keep in mind the hardships of military service, they concentrated not on functional characteristics but on the symbolism of the new uniform.

The name of the true author of the Red Army uniform is not known. It could possibly have been a group of artists, with the commission choosing the most suitable elements from each. The first prize in the contest is known to have been awarded to artist S. Arkadievsky, who was thereafter entrusted with the execution of the entire project.

Like the artists who made decorations for the first revolutionary holidays, the designers strove to incarnate the dream of a romantic, heroic warrior, the defender of revolutionary ideals. They tried to invent a system of symbols capable of imparting a special meaning to the soldier's ordinary uniform. The contestants seemed unconsciously to have set themselves the tasks peculiar to art and were trying to accomplish them through the language of an artistic image.

Among the designers of the new Red Army uniform was the famous painter Boris Kustodiyev. His daughter Irina recounts: "My brother and I remember that soon after the October Revolution, father received an offer from the Revolutionary Military Council to sketch a uniform for the Red Army men. He made several versions, suggesting, in part, a helmet that

25

26

27

26
M. Cheremnykh. *A Tale of a Red Army Man...* poster. 1922. Displays the details of the Red Army uniform.

27
V. I. Chapaiev and S. I. Zakharov, Division Commander, at the Nikolaevsk-Uralsky station in 1919.

28
Woman worker's clothes. 1920-1921.

29
Red Army uniform: the helmet with a star and the greatcoat with the so-called *razgovory*, or decorative stripes, including those with buttonholes. 1919.

7.
B. M. Kustodiyev. *Sbornik pisem i vospominanii*. Moscow, Khudozhnik RSFSR, 1967, p. 319.

resembled the old Russian one. The sketches were sent to Moscow, but no answer came."[7]

The allure of a heroic epic image led the designers of the uniform to the clothes of the old Russian army of Prince Dmitri Donskoi's times, the epoch associated in the national memory with the Russian struggle against foreign invasion and for independence. Such an analogy naturally suggested itself in the stormy revolutionary days of the defense of the young Soviet republic from foreign and domestic enemies. The artists thus came up with a helmet resembling the pointed steel helmets of the Russian warriors of the 15th century. Their sketches evolved through studying historical documents in the archives of the Armory in the Moscow Kremlin and of the History Museum.

On 18 December 1918, the Revolutionary Military Council of the Republic approved a new military uniform for the Red Army soldiers. The headgear was a helmet covered in khaki with a five-pointed star (its color depended on the branch of the service). In the center of the helmet above the star was a cockade depicting a hammer and a plough symbolizing the union of the workers and the peasants. Initially the helmet was called a *bogatyrka*, since it resembled the headgear of the Russian folklore hero with this name. But, when the helmet was included in the uniform of

Semen Budennyi's division, the name *budenovka* began to be used.

In April 1919 other elements of the dress appeared: the greatcoat, shirt, and leather shoes made of bast (a fibrous material used for rope). Modified forms of Russian folk clothes could be seen in the uniform. The similarity is noticeable not only in the headgear but also in the construction of the greatcoat, which was similar to a caftan in shape, with its silhouette slightly fitted at the waist and its double-breasted fastening. This time designers met the requirements of the contest — to make the military uniform comfortable and warm. Earflaps were added to the helmet, and the greatcoat was made of a special thick cloth.

The image of the uniform was created with well thought-out decorative accents. The message it projected depended, above all on the color red, the hue of the revolutionary banner: it blazed on the star of the helmet and lined the buttonholes and the cuffs of the greatcoat sleeves. The language of symbol here was precise and effective. At the same time the subordination to the new uniform's symbolic image somewhat reduced its functional characteristics. The first greatcoats with red stripes on the left side of the breast, dubbed *razgovory* (conversations), were introduced in 1919. They were accompanied by the summer uniform: a shirt with *razgovory* on the collar and the breast. Since low industrial production capacities did not allow the entire personnel of the Red Army to be supplied with the new outfit, after the end of the Civil War attention again turned toward a single uniform for the Red Army soldiers.

In January 1922 a new uniform for all arms of the service was introduced by the decree of the Revolutionary Military Council of the Republic. All servicemen were provided with gray greatcoats, winter and summer shirts, winter helmets and summer caps.

In subsequent years the Red Army uniform gradually parted with decorative details and with the color red. Military dress became increasingly simple and utilitarian. The *budenovka* helmet alone lived to see the Second World War, but it was soon replaced by a cap with earflaps.

The Red Army uniform was a turning point in the history of Soviet design.[8] Even today, decades later, when recalling the epoch of the Great October Revolution, we associate it first of all with the figure of a heroic Red Army soldier in a greatcoat with *razgovory* and a *budenovka* with a red star — an association that testifies to the symbolic power of the art of clothing design.

8.
As a salute to the earlier revolutionary epoch, the form of the greatcoat and helmet was revived in Soviet design in 1967 on the eve of the 50th anniversary of the October Revolution. It was not, however, a copy of the old models but rather a creative reminder, an echo of military uniform motifs, this time in a fashionable ensemble of a woman's dress.

30

D. Moor. *I Am an Atheist.*
Subscription advertisement for
the magazine *Bezbozhnik* (The
Atheist). 1925.

31

D. Moor. *The oath taken when
joining the Workers' and Peasants'
Red Army,* poster. 1918.

32
N. Suetin. *A Woman with a Saw*.
1920s.

33
K. Malevich. Sketch of a dress.
1923.

The First Steps

The reconstruction of the country's economic base began in the months following the October Revolution, an extremely difficult and dangerous period. The collapse of the economy due to the protracted world war, the beginning civil war and foreign intervention jeopardized the very existence of the Soviet state. Nevertheless, it was at that time that colossal work began on the launching of new Soviet institutions in the various branches of the national economy, including the garment industry.

Feudal-type production by craftsmen was no longer adequate to the needs of the new society. The entire system had to be restructured, eliminating, first of all, the hundreds of small garment workshops and directing energy and labor toward industrial production. This complicated task was entrusted in mid-1918 to the Ready-Made Clothes and Linen Section of the Central Textile Department "to restore, unify and nationalize the manufacture and distribution of ready-made clothes and linen on a national scale."[9]

In April 1919 the section was made an independent industry, to be directed by the Central Committee of the Garment Industry under the All-Russian Council of National Economy. The charter of its organization

9.
The decision of the Central Textile Department is quoted from V. Popkov, "Industrialnaia shveinaia promyshlennost — detishche Velikogo Oktiabria" in *Shveinaia promyshlennost*, 1967, no. 1, p. 21.

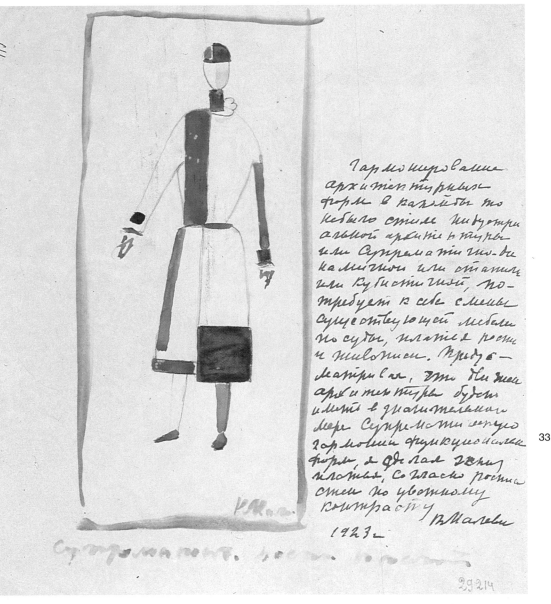

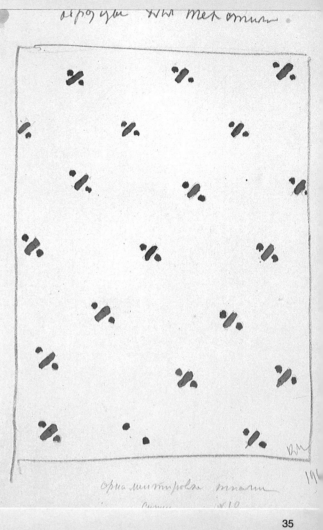

34
Fabric made after K. Malevich's design. Showing the sample at exhibitions, Kazimir Malevich supplied his own inscription: "The first fabric of suprematist ornamentation produced in Vitebsk in 1919."

35-38
K. Malevich. Fabric designs. 1919. Prior to the Revolution, Malevich formulated the conception of suprematism, the acme of human art. In 1919 in Vitebsk he began practically applying his ideas with a group of disciples. They created "architectons," which were models of houses of the future, projects for murals, and "ornamentation of fabrics."

34

35

structure and responsibilities was signed by Rykov, the Chairman of the Council, and two members of the Council's Presidium: V. Miliutin and V. Nogin. First, organizations for the mass production of garments were created: Moskvoshvei in Moscow and Leningradshvei in Leningrad, with eight more enterprises located in big cities. Most of them worked for the army. The transformation of a huge branch of small-scale commodity production into a socialist industry could not proceed smoothly — that is clear from archival documents, including those of the Central State Archives of the National Economy (TsGANKh). No doubt the organizational restructuring, far from improving the situation, had made it even worse, for it required a fundamental change in the existing economic system.

In addition, the management of economic structures in 1918-1919 was unstable. Too many factors influenced the planners' work, sometimes bringing to naught the most promising and far-sighted projects. The TsGANKh literature contains an analysis by a commission that examined the possibilities of establishing a central committee. The commission concluded that the garment industry would be virtually impossible to nationalize: "The disastrous growth of prices on foodstuffs and other goods has reduced market capacity to a minimum and the garment industry to almost complete annihilation.

36 37 38

39

39

K. Malevich. Sketch of a dress,
1923. In the world that Malevich
undertook to remake with his art,
everything was to be in harmony
—the design of fabrics and the
clothes made from them, murals
and their buildings. Clothes were
part of the general "ensemble of
forms," and Malevich thought that
every artist should contribute to it.

1. The ratio between factory garment production and small workshop production is one to a hundred.

2. There is no division of labor at the factories; nonetheless, specialization of production is absolutely essential.

10.
TsGANKh, f. 3338, op. 5, d. 19.

3. There is no industrialization."[10]

It required courage, indeed, to try to convert this huge, backward branch of production into a socialized industry. In spite of all this, it was decided to carry through the nationalization. In August of the same year, the Central Committee of the Garment Industry was dissolved and its functions were transferred to other organizations. Central among them was the Clothes Chief Directorate, with a network of independent Provincial Clothes Chief Directorates. In its charge "all nationalized garment enterprises and all small factories, handicraft workshops, cooperative and artel [collective] enterprises, of both garment-making, preparatory (cut-

11.
TsGANKh, f. 803, op. 1, d. 7.

ting) and distributing types."[11]

The organizational measures did not immediately alter the character of the garment industry; in fact the process lasted approximately to the mid-1930s. In the early 1920s, production of textiles and clothes sharply declined. Textile goods shortages were severe — before 1924, the variety and quality of textiles in general left much to be desired. Most were unprinted fabrics: linen canvas, cloth, tarpaulin, soldier's cloth, low-grade woollens, thick flannelette, coarse calico and cotton.

The Clothes Chief Directorate contained within its system a special Chief Administrative Board for the production of military uniforms, work and civilian clothes. Factories supplied the most urgently needed types of work clothes: tarpaulin cloaks, overalls, men's shirts, and women's blouses and skirts, all of them designed along functional lines and without embellishment.

12.
The newspaper Zhizn iskusstva, 23 January 1919.

In January 1919, the artists' trade union announced a contest for a design of workers' houses and "also sketches of suits, a dress, an apron, etc."[12] The artists believed that through an integral creative approach to the problem of the residential environment, they could develop an appreciation of good design in the masses.

The most important event in the creation of new forms of clothing was

13.
They were initially called
the Industrial Costume Art
Studio.

14.
In 1969 the archives were
given to me by Nadezhda
Lamanova's niece, N. Krakht.

15.
*Protokoly Pervoi vserossiiskoi
konferentsii po khudozhest-
vennoi promyshlennosti.*
Moscow, 1920, pp. 3738.

16.
MOAORS, f. 967, op. 1, d. 88
(a copy).

the opening of Workshops of Contemporary Dress[13] under the industrial-art subsection of the People's Commissariat for Public Education Fine Arts Section (IZO Narkompros). The idea of the Workshops was suggested by Nadezhda Lamanova, a widely known artist and professional clothing designer. Lamanova made her proposal early in 1919 to the People's Commissar of Public Education A. Lunacharsky, and wrote a detailed syllabus for the Workshops of Contemporary Dress.[14]

The IZO Narkompros industrial-art subsection consisted of several units: a modern costume laboratory and industrial training workshop, a man's suit tailoring industrial-art workshop, an industrial textile workshop, and a cotton-printing workshop under the former Prokhorovskaia, later Trekhgornaia, textile mill. Thus the structural division of the units reflected the main thrust of the work: instruction in the fundamentals of the new costume design, in the dressmaking and tailoring trade, and in the relation between the form of costume and the nature of the fabric: its texture and ornamental design. Lamanova stressed, moreover, by the word "industrial," that the work had as its target industrial mass production. She expressed her view of the costume designer's role at the first All-Russian Art Industry Conference in August 1919. "Art must penetrate all spheres of life, and develop an artistic taste in the masses. Clothes are one of the most suitable areas. . . . Artists must take the initiative, working to create from plain fabrics simple but beautiful garments befitting the new mode of working life."[15]

The Workshops of Contemporary Dress became a creative laboratory. Simultaneously, again with Lamanova's participation, a program was drafted for the first Soviet educational establishments that were to train specialists for the garment industry, since the absence of experts hampered, and in fact prevented, the development of this vast branch of light industry. Thus in January 1919 the Central Institute of the Garment Industry was born.[16] The People's Commissariat of Commerce and Industry said in its report about the organization: "The Central Institute of the Garment Industry has been created to perform two main tasks: first, to research and solve all problems, through scientific studies and practical experiments, of scientific organization of production and work, of the

40

Yu. Pimenov. *We Are Building...*
1920. The drawing reveals the
constructive spirit of 1920s art.
Factories and plants, clubs for the
workers, and stadiums were being
built, the new way of life was
being created, and the New Man
was believed to be coming into
existence.

Пролетарии всех стран, соединяйтесь!

ТЫ

ЗАПИСАЛСЯ
ДОБРОВОЛЬЦЕМ?

41

41
D. Moor. *Have You Volunteered for the Red Army?* poster. 1920.

42
A. Samokhvalov. *Guarding her Motherland.* 1920.
The marvelous new world of universal brotherhood and prosperity visualized by the theorists was yet to be built. In the 1920s this optimistic idea had to be defended. Both men and women took up arms. The 1920 poster called upon the working people to volunteer for the army, though in 1918 compulsory military service had already been introduced.

introduction of hygienic and artistically-designed clothes, and of methods of instruction at vocational training institutions; and secondly, to train technical organizers and managers for the industry as well as instructors who possess expert knowledge."[17] In the statutes of the Central Institute of the Garment Industry it was described as a higher scientific and educational institution, although its course of instruction lasted only four to six semesters. Nevertheless, its program provided an extensive coverage of specialized subjects.

"The complete absence of textbooks and necessary materials in all branches of education in the garment industry makes it necessary to classify the existing materials on the organization of factory production, to write special literature — textbooks and reference books — and to devise better methods of organization of production and instruction."[18] This program for the Central Institute was established under the Chief Committee for Vocational Training. The problem of designing new forms of clothes for the citizenry was to be solved through a combination of artistic, economic, and organizational measures. The Institute was to collect information on the history of the garment industry and on the industrial geography of Russia and other countries.[19]

The Sokolniki Soviet Educational Industrial Art Studios of Costume also opened in Moscow in 1919 under the same People's Commissariat of Commerce and Industry. Artist Mikhail Tarkhanov was made head of the Studios. Its agenda had much in common with that of the Central Institute, with several differences: the Studios envisaged greater contact with the industry and with other clothes-producing organizations. The course of instruction included the many techniques of garment-making and the history of art, cutting, drawing, account-

17.
Ibid.

18.
GAMO, f. 967, op. 1, d. 88.

19.
Ibid.

42

43

Servicemen at a health resort,
1928. The unvarying summer
clothes of while linen resemble
a uniform.

44, 45

The garments of professionals in
the 1920s were more individualized.
Note the elegant clothes worn by
Esfir Shub (left), the film director
and friend of Sergei Eisenstein,
author of the documentaries *The
Fall of the Romanov Dynasty*, *The
Land of Soviets*, and *Spain*, and
the actress Roshchin-Insarov.

43

44

45

ing, occupational hygiene and labor legislation. The students were given the opportunity to tour their own country and abroad. The term of study lasted three years.

The Studios' program stressed the importance of keeping in touch "both with local industry and with individual organizations and exemplary workshops, museums of industrial and applied arts, fine arts societies, trade unions of producers, state art studios, etc."[20] Such a wide and diversified range of instruction was essential to produce specialists with a profound knowledge of their trade, and prepare them for working in the different spheres of garment production.

These schools were a direct result of the extensive campaign that encouraged artists to renew all branches of art industry. The vitality of the arts sector in those years was demonstrated by the demand from the public and senior officials of the Textile Chief Directorate for a museum of textile industry, which would display the best samples of that time as well as recount the history of Russian textiles, and thus constitute a showcase of achievements in this field.[21] Unfortunately, this proposal was never realized, and no textile museum of national importance was ever established in the USSR.

20.
GAMO, f. 867, op. 1, d. 88.

21.
TsGANKh, f. 3338, op. 5, d. 90.

46

47

48

49

The Attitude Toward "Fashion" in the Early 1920s

The October Revolution eliminated the class differentiation of clothing that had existed in Russia for centuries, and introduced the concept of a mass costume for the working people. Differences between citizens were still indicated by dress, but were now due to factors such as living and working conditions, climate, age, and cultural and ethnic traditions. Real progress in the creation of clothing for the people, however, was hampered by many problems. The principal ones were the backwardness of the industry, the lack of garment industry specialists, and the reluctance of the masses to accept the idea of fashionable clothes.

The variety of clothes produced during the years 1918-1921 was extremely limited. The impoverished people, exhausted by civil war and widespread famine, wore old garments that they frequently patched and altered, using as material anything they could lay their hands on: tablecloths, curtains, blankets, etc.

At the same time, many of the old types of clothes acquired a new meaning: the leather jacket commonly used as a driver's uniform before

50

46-49
Yu. Razumavskaia. *The sort of people you meet in the streets of Moscow.* 1920.

50
Yu. Vakhrameiev. *An Arm of the Law.* 1920. In the years of Civil War, famine, and economic dislocation, one could often see in Moscow and other big cities peasant women in coats of heavy cloth and sheepskins, wrapped in shawls. The government had prohibited private trade and begun centralized distribution of goods. But no decrees could prevent the peasant woman from bartering eggs, butter, and port for nails, thread, and fabrics. "The are of the law," to all appearances a peasant woman, had among her other duties that of suppressing "speculation."

51

K. Vialov. *The Militiaman*. 1923.
The uniform of the People's
Militia, designed by the artist
himself, is drawn in detail.

52

S. Adlivankin. *Tram B*. 1922.
A parade of garments of all
classes, which became equal in
the face of transport problems.

the revolution became popular as the ''work clothes'' of Red Army commissars and Party leaders. Still in favor were Tolstoy-style shirts and elements of military clothes: service jackets, high boots, and wide leather belts; women made dresses of rough one-color fabrics. Despite the shortage of textiles and complete absence of the notion of ''fashion,'' the appearance of the people reflected the ''style of the time'' — it was austere and tired, but in fighting trim. This is strikingly clear in the photographs of that time and in the paintings of Mitrofan Grekov, Alexandr Samokhvalov, Kuzma Petrov-Vodkin, and Alexandr Deineka.

The problems of costume gave rise to furious polemics. A fierce struggle was being waged on the front line of arts, with clashes taking place not between enemies but between people sharing the same values and beliefs. There was a prevailing desire to destroy the old world, and with it its entire culture. Characteristically, prerevolutionary culture was identified with a bourgeois ideology, which was alien and hostile to socialism, and discussions of a new costume acquired a vehement character.

53

54

53
B. Kustodiev. *Lengiz* (Leningrad Branch of the State Publishing House). Poster. 1925.

54
B. Kustodiev. Sketch of the poster *Alliance Between Town and Country*. 1925. The alliance between the workers and the peasants announced in theory did not exist. The revolution gave land to the peasants but took from them all their grain to feed the workers and the army. In propaganda arts the alliance between town and country was presented as the enlightenment of the people, as the exchange of books, whereas the "alliance" was actually achieved through trade permitted during the New Economic Policy (NEP) and the abolition of grain requisitioning. The bearded peasant and his son in Kustodiev's poster are clothed in sheepskins and felt boots, which were worn in winter all over Russia for centuries.

Most people were utterly unprepared to accept the idea of fashionable clothes for ordinary citizens — there certainly was no precedent for it in the past. Therefore the years immediately following the October Revolution were full of confusion and conflict. The very word "fashionable" became tantamount to an insult. This prejudice was understandable: fashion had always been associated with bourgeois society; it signified privileges for the select few. To deny fashion was to deny the luxurious attire of the bourgeoisie and anything resembling membership to an elite. For almost a decade after the Revolution, "fashion" was synonymous with impermissible luxury, frivolity, and quite extravagant decoration.

"Fashion" was interpreted as brightly colored neckties and shirts and women's dresses decorated with frills or lace. Even hats and briefcases were branded "bourgeois accessories." The proletarian concept of socialist garments was that they should be as simple as possible, almost puritanical. The situation was complicated by the diverse interpretations of the "truly socialist" forms of the new costume, many of which were diametrically opposed.

Magazines published in 1919-1920 provided a platform for heated debates on the new way of life and the necessity of radical change in mass-produced clothes. V. Kerzhentsev's article, "A Rebuke to Artists," posed the following question: "Is there in Soviet Russia at least one artist who will seriously consider replacing our ridiculous, vulgar, petty-bourgeois costume with something new, truly beautiful, elegantly cut, and attractively colored? It is high time we discarded our black-to-blue and grey-to-green gamut of men's suits and our preposterous peaked caps and bowler hats. Let artists create models of a new costume that reflects the riot of color of the Revolution and its democracy. Some forms of blouse might take, at last, the place of coats and waistcoats. Maybe a new variety of Phrygian cap [again an association with the French Revolution] will be produced for us by the artist's imagination. . . ."

"So far fashions have been created by the manufacturer with the help of his assistants. Let fashion now be taken in hand by genuine artists, who have beauty as their aim and who take into account all the peculiarities of our life and the nature of modern production. Why shouldn't the fine arts section begin publishing a fashion magazine, which could develop the ideas of a new costume? I would prefer, I must confess, such a publication even to Kandinsky's fine book!''[22]

22.
The newspaper *Sovetskaia strana*, 10 February 1919.

Many different societies began to appear, each proposing its own principles on clothing. The most extraordinary among them was the Away with Shame Society. Their outrageously bright carnivalesque outfits startled the poor, drably dressed people in the streets. These ''ultrarevolutionaries'' exhibited a nihilistic attitude toward tradition, but they were probably more interested in attracting attention through Dada-like *gestes* than in truly influencing fashion.

The following account published in the newspaper *Zhizn iskusstva* (The Life of Art) vividly recreates the atmosphere of the time and presents the main principles of the new costume: ''The first conference took place in the building of the Commissariat of Public Health to discuss the creation of a new work costume that fufilled present-day requirements. Invited to the conference were specialists in art, medicine, technology, etc. The group that has decided to create new work clothes believes that the

56
57

55

I. Vladimirov. *Photographer in a Village.* 1928.

56

E. Cheptsov. *Meeting of the Village Party Cell.* 1924.

57

S. Maliutin. *Portrait of D. Furmanov, Commissar of the Chapaiev Division.* 1922.

Vladimirov's painting shows traditional peasant clothes: women in wide skirts, practical blouses made of homespun linen. The young couple in front of the camera are dressed in town clothes. The girl wears a silk dress, the boy wears a coat. In the 1920s many newcomers appeared in the countryside wearing half-urban, half-military clothes: soldier's blouses, boots and leather jackets. They were workers from factories that were standing idle, and had come to find food and to survive the hard times. Then arrived the agitators and active workers sent by the Party through whom collectivization of agriculture was later carried through.

58

A. Samokhvalov. *Girl in a Football Jersey*. 1932. The striped football jersey was one of the most widespread types of urban clothes in the 1920s and the 1930s. A girl could wear such a jersey on both a tennis and volley-ball court; they were worn by participants in physical culture parades and by amateur actors on the stages of clubs and theaters. One-third of the manufactured knitted fabrics at this time were made of cotton and intended for sports clothes. The *Girl in a Football Jersey* was the ideal of beauty in the 1920s and 1930s. Describing the heroine of *The Golden Calf*, the authors of this popular novel, Ilia Ilf and Evgeni Petrov, wrote that she looked "athletic, like all beautiful girls of that time."

59

Young women workers of the knitwear factory in Kosino near Moscow who won a track-and-field athletics competition. 1926.

58

59

existing work dress — the worker's blouse — is not rational enough. The great Russian revolution must have its influence on the outer as well as the inner man. The new clothes must not only be comfortable and elegant but must be fully dependent on economic conditions and answer hygienic requirements."[23] This was typical of the attention given at this time to the functional aspect of clothing, which depended greatly on one's line of trade and working conditions, and to the importance attributed to work clothes over other garments.

23.
"Rabochii kostium" in *Zhizn iskusstva*, 1919, no. 142, p. 1.

The decision of the Labor and Defense Council dated 8 October 1920 and signed by its Chairman Ulianov (Lenin) "On the Provision with *Prozodezhda* and *Spetsodezhda* of Workers in Coal Mines" introduced the concept of *prozodezhda*. This was slightly less confining than *spetsodezhda* (specific jobs requiring specific dress): it designated clothing for the working man of a specific category, whether for labor, relaxation, etc. It merged to a large extent with efforts to bring everyday garments, women's in particular, closer to sportswear. Introducing sport clothes into everyday life was a frequent topic of discussion in newspapers and magazines. The articles, usually written by journalists, contained many passionate appeals and descriptions, sometimes quite naive, of the ideal sportswear style. T. Khoks, in her article "Organization of the Body," fiercely attacked the dull, uninspired clothes of the citizenry. They "hinder movements and are unhygienic . . . their shapes are meaningless . . . a harmful effect on the organism is produced by the tight and uncomfortable footwear. . . . The form of costume is dictated by 'beauty' and by custom, but in no way by expediency. . . . Last summer shorts were worn in the city not only by organized groups in processions but also by individuals. The first attack on the suit has been made."[24]

24.
T. Khoks, "Organizatsia tela" in *Oktiabr mysli*, 1924, no. 2, pp. 61-62.

Fashion even attracted the attention of the *belles-lettristes* who have provided us with a vivid picture of the 1920s. In his feature story "On High Living," Pavel Nili wrote: "Kostia Zaitsev bought silk pyjamas with sky-blue satin lapels at the second-hand market in Rostov. He then went to the steppe. And in the morning his behavior was discussed by the bureau of the Komsomol (Young Communist League): 'K. Zaitsev, a Komsomol member, is degenerating before our very eyes.' 'It means losing touch with the masses,' said Gromov, secretary of the bureau and a coal cutter, when it was discovered during the debate that besides the pyjamas Zaitsev had also acquired a felt hat, a dotted crimson necktie and yellow gaiters. 'An intellectual, indeed!' The Party secretary defended Zaitsev but advised him not to wear the pyjamas. 'You are overhasty. . . . And this is wrong. The masses think you are a crank . . . an eccentric . . . and you are a member, as you know, of this bureau. You see it's quite improper.' Zaitsev hid the pyjamas in a trunk.''[25]

25.
P. Nilin, ''O roskoshnoi zhizni'' in *Nashi dostizhenia*, no. 6, 1934, pp. 56-57.

60

60

A. Strakhov. *Emancipated Women Build Socialism!* Poster. 1926.

61

A. Deineka. *Building New Workshops*. 1926. Prior to the revolution, women who were employed in factories worked mainly in the textile industry.

The revolution gave women equal rights with men. The "emancipated" women began to operate machines, drive trucks and work as builders. The image of a woman with a hammer, often seen on posters of that era, was not merely a metaphor.

The Revival of the Garment Industry

Despite the resolute measures to reorganize the garment industry in the 1920s, it proved impossible to end the textile goods shortage in the country and to provide the population with industrially produced clothing. During this decade the majority of garments were provided by the private tailor and amateur dressmaker, who in many cases obstinately copied prerevolutionary fashion, with a few desultory personal touches.

By the end of 1921, military clothing orders were down, and with the transition to the New Economic Policy (NEP), the balance between the output of military and civilian clothes changed in favor of the latter. The primitive machinery in the factories had long slowed the progress of production, and was gradually replaced by presses of new design, gas irons, and other up-to-date equipment purchased abroad. These measures allowed mass clothes to be produced more cheaply and also raised labor productivity.

The first Soviet garment factories were extremely dissimilar in terms of technical facilities and personnel. One enterprise might have the latest electric sewing machines from America and very old treadle or hand operated machines working side by side, and in the adjoining shop minor

62
D. Shterenberg. *Portrait of the Artist's Wife.* 1925-1926.

63
B. Kustodiev. *Portrait of L. Gatsuk-Orshanskaia.* 1926. Women in artistic circles retained interest in fashions, still had dresses and maintained contact with dressmakers. The dress of L. Gatsuk-Orshanskaia — long-waisted, of heavy silk — is irreproachably elegant, in keeping with the last word in European fashion of that time, and perhaps made by an experienced dressmaker who had studied the latest Paris fashion magazines.

63

64
B. Kustodiev. *Portrait of N. Orshanskaia.* 1925.

65
B. Kustodiev. *Singing to My Darling's Music.* 1927.

66
G. B. Kustodiev. *Portrait of Yu. Kustodieva.* 1927.

N. Orshanskaia's interest in art is clear not only from the pictures on the walls of her home but also from her garments. The dress of refined simplicity is supplemented with a shawl decorated with a modern geometric design. The attire seems quite unusual. The garb of the factory girl combines the uncombinable: striped stockings and a gay-colored dress, a proletarian kerchief on her head and a patterned shawl of a peasant woman on her shoulders. The clothes of a "progressive" intellectual are severe and modest, the checked pattern of the dress is emphatically workaday.

67
V. Lebedev. *The Ironer.* 1925.

64

65
66

operations like sewing on and overstitching buttons were done by hand. These combinations of technical levels led to the division of the shops into "ancient, middle-aged and modern." Specialized labor was in short supply, therefore quite a few inexperienced workers were hired. There was no time to train this first generation of garment makers, so people of different ages, character and background had to plunge into the vortex of production and learn while working, adapting themselves to the new rhythm of life and the new conditions and relationships of the work collective.

During the New Economic Policy period (1921-1928), contacts with Parisian fashion that had been interrupted by the revolution were re-established. French fashion magazines were again on sale, and Soviet ones were created: in 1922, *Novosti mod. Khudozhestvenny ezhemesiachnyi zhurnal poslednikh parizhskikh mod* (Fashion News: Pictorial Monthly of Current Parisian Fashion); in 1923, *Poslednie mody. Zhurnal dlia zhenshchin* (The Latest Fashions: A Magazine for Women); and in 1924, *Mody* (Fashion). These Soviet periodicals were filled with pic-

tures of expensive dresses reflecting the tastes of the French bourgeoisie. Stylistically they resembled modern design. The dresses were of the so-called "bird silhouette": elongated, tight-fitting, with a *vandyke* skirt, a complicated cut and numerous decorative details. They were made of expensive fabrics: silk, brocade, velvet and often a combination of materials. The bird silhouette was enhanced by a tiny hat perched over one eye. The ensembles often had matching footwear; frequently narrow-toed shoes with a strap. The high price tags of these clothes confirmed their elite nature, and they obviously catered to a narrow circle of wealthy clients, specifically the NEP bourgeoisie.

68

69

70

68
Yu. Ganf. Caricature from the satirical review *Krokodil* (The Crocodile) of 1927.

69
S. Zaklikovskaia. *The Old and the New Way of Life*. 1927.

70
A chorus in front of the Bolshoi Theater in Moscow. 1921.

71
May Day demonstration in Moscow. 1925. Heated debates about the old and the new way of life were carried on in the 1920s, and not only in the newspapers. The struggle also flared up in drawings and paintings. In conformity with the formula "being determines consciousness," the new way of life was to bring into existence a new kind of man. The new man wears simple, comfortable clothes, after work plays chess at a workers' club, when alone is occupied with political self-education, and takes part in mass holidays and other totalitarian entertainments. The clergy, drunken peasants and decadent idlers leading a dissipated life all belong to the past. Clothes served as a code for distinguishing between people of the past and of the future.

In striking contrast were the everyday clothes of working women, who wore cheap cotton dresses, sports jerseys with wide vertical stripes, and straight or slightly flared short skirts. As simple, and almost primitive, were men's outfits consisting of sports jerseys or shirts and wide shapeless trousers. The main footwear were plimsolls (rubber-soled canvas sports shoes). These clothes were almost impossible to classify as fashionable. True, a stylish woman's wardrobe included a long skirt, which had something in common with the fashion of that period and whose cut was reminiscent of early 20th-century clothes design.

Thus mass clothes in the NEP period as well were limited to a small range of garments. Nevertheless, in apparel, as in state policy and culture, there could be no turning back. The slight but growing interest in foreign fashions had little influence on the new principles of Soviet costume that were beginning to take root. Moreover, the burgeoning revival of the economy in the NEP period boosted cultural progress —

72

it was during this time that the most decisive steps were taken to work out the principles of Soviet garment design. The atmosphere of peace and the consolidation of the production base finally encouraged concrete projects for mass-produced clothing, and the Atelier of Fashions was opened in 1923 at the Moscow Garment-Producing Trust. The Atelier was regarded as the theoretical and ideological center of the art of fashion design — a sort of prototype of the future House of Clothing Design. It began publication of the magazine *Atelier*. The importance attached to this journal can be seen from the composition of its editorial board. B. Kustodiev, I. Grabar, A. Golovin, V. Mukhina, K. Petrov-Vodkin, K. Yuon, E. Pribylskaia,

73

74

72

G. Riazhsky. *A Delegate.* 1927.

73

P. Konchalovsky. *Portrait of Konchalovskaia.* 1925.

74

S. Bogdanov. *The Seamstresses.* 1925.

The Soviet women received equal rights with men, the right to vote and the right to express their views. The delegate's clothes are the model of proletarian ''elegance'': a simple blouse and skirt and a red kerchief. The wife of an artist, writer, or scientist patronized by the authorities could wear expensive silk garments, elegant shoes and live in obviously non-proletarian surroundings. On the other hand, the majority of women who were not enamored of the proletarian Puritanism in clothes spent much time bent over a sewing machine.

75

76

75

V. Perelman. *The Worker Correspondent.* 1925.

76

A. Volter. *Portrait of a Red Military Pilot.* 1924.

77

Yu. Pimenov. *Portrait of Architect Burov.* 1928. We see here the elite of the new society: a journalist, a pilot and an architect. Their clothes have almost nothing in common. Clothes in the 1920s to a considerable extent lost their function of social differentiation. For example, prior to the revolution leather jackets were worn by drivers serving wealthy employers. After the revolution, the leather jacket acquired a symbolic meaning. "Leather jackets" denoted Bolsheviks (as in Boris Pilniak's novel *The Year of Famine*) and later Cheka officials and commissars in the army. The worker correspondent informs the masses of Party directives. He wears a leather jacket, the uniform of people who think as he does.

N. Lamanova, A. Exter, I. Fomin, A. Akhmatova, K. Fedin, O. Forsh, M. Shaginian and many other eminent writers, artists, and architects. The editorial in the first issue of the journal described its goals: "It is now quite clear that art should be used in practical matters and in the different branches of our reviving industry. The vigorous creative activities of Russian artists should be the source of new forms. Today, refinement and harmony in our everyday surroundings should be created by the joint efforts of artists and managers of contemporary industry — through a search for beauty on the part of the artists and the practical achievements of industrialists. To reveal everything that is creatively beautiful, that deserves attention in the field of material culture: this is the purpose of the present journal."[26]

26.
Atelier, 1923, no. 1, p. 3.

The illustrations — the latest fashions by leading designers — were not the only subjects of interest in the magazine. No less important were its articles: A. Exter, "Constructive Clothing"; E. Pribylskaia, "Embroidery in Present-Day Manufacture"; V. von Meck, "Costume and the Revolution"; M. Kuzmin, "The Influence of Costume on Theatrical Productions"; V. Izvitsky, "The Exhibition of Art Industry in Moscow in 1923"; P. Trifonov, "Five Years of Moskvoshvei's Activities"; and N. Ivanov, "Silk". The very titles of the articles reflect an attempt to embrace the diverse aspects of creative new clothing design and their relation to life, sociology, and culture. The magazine also gave the historical background of the evolution of the Russian garment industry and described the practical tasks of the Atelier of Fashions. The Atelier was to accomplish two tasks: first, create models of daily clothes for mass production, and, second, make garments to order. Analysis of the two tasks is quite instructive, and reveals two distinct branches of development in the art of

77

78

78
I. Mashkov. *Lady in a Blue Dress.*
1927.

79
L. Akashin. *A Family Portrait.*
1931.

80
G. Riazhsky. *The Chairwoman.*
1928. Ten years had passed since
the proletarian revolution, but
class distinctions remained: the
portrait of a lady sitting in an arm-
chair surrounded with antique
objects is evidence of that. The
chairwoman of a collective farm,
a village activist, is clothed in a
peasant sheepskin. In such a
sheepskin the builder of the new
life in the countryside both
presided over a meeting in a
peasant's log cabin to discuss
farming matters, and mounted the
platform of the unheated Bolshoi
Theater, where congresses of
Soviets often adjourned.

79

Soviet clothing design. For the first time the possibility of creating garments combining fashionable trends with tradition (E. Pribylskaia, P. Trifonov) was discussed. The authors proposed using the designs of folk clothes not only for decorative purposes but also to mold a distinctive Soviet costume.

The illustrations featured dresses by N. Lamanova, A. Exter, E. Pribylskaia, and V. Mukhina. There was an obvious discrepancy, however, between the text of the articles and the illustrations. The articles urged artists to design clothing that could be produced in large quantities for the working people, but that nevertheless possessed high artistic merits; whereas the illustrations exhibited primarily expensive, almost aristocratic clothes. This journal lasted only one year: its bias toward elitism was seen as contradicting the principles of the new society.

Atelier's functions were assumed by other institutions and periodicals. These included the Workshops of Contemporary Dress under the direction of N. Lamanova, opened in the same year of 1923, the costume section of the State Academy of Artistic Sciences (GAKhN), where V. Stepanova taught, and also the journals *Iskusstvo* and *Krasnaia niva* ("Red Fields"), among other publications.

A major event of 1923 was the display of garments designed by artists

of the Atelier workshops at the First All-Russian Industrial Art Exhibition arranged by the GAKhN. It was then that the public first heard the names of the earliest Soviet dress designers, artists of diverse personalities and styles: N. Lamanova, E. Pribylskaia, V. Mukhina, A. Exter. For this show the artists created a number of ornaments from unusual materials such as peas and bast. The authors' skillful craftsmanship and imagination, however, made these ornaments quite modern and finely executed works of art.

81

81

Portrait of young Nadezhda
Lamanova. 1880s.

82

Nadezhda Lamanova. 1910.
A dress-designer for the royal
court, Lamanova kept designing
after the revolution of October
1917, experiencing in her declining
years a resurgence of her creative
powers. She dedicated herself to
the creation of mass clothes for
the people of the "marvelous
new world."

Nadezhda Lamanova (1861-1941)

Autobiography

I was born on 14 December 1861. I
attended the well-known dressmaking
school of O. A. Suvorova (1883), and in
1884-1885 worked for hire as a designer
at Voitkevich's dressmaking establishment. From 1885 to 1917 I had a dressmaking establishment of my own.
I began working for the Moscow Art
Theater in 1901, and made costumes for
the play *In Dreams* by V. I. Nemirovich-
Danchenko, and *The Cherry Orchard*. In
1918 I joined the Art Workers' Union and
again worked for the Art Theater.

From 1919, I was head of the State
Training and Manufacturing Workshop of
Costume at the Art Industry Department
of the People's Commissariat of Public
Education of the RSFSR, under the
Central Science Board, and
simultaneously an artistic modelling
instructor at the Igla (Needle) Section of
thee Moscow Public Education
Department. During that period I
organized three exhibitions. In 1921 I
began working at the Vakhtangov
Theater, where I have been working for
sixteen years. I have constructed
costumes for the following plays:
Turandot (the costumes are altered every
one or two years), *Zoika's Flat, The
Daughter of a Russian Actor, On Blood,
Marion de Lorm, Kable und Liebe, Egor
Bulychev, Dostigaiev and Others, The
Envy, Hamlet, The Human Comedy,
Florisdorf, Much Ado About Nothing*,
and *Guilty Though Guiltless*.
I also work at the Griboedov Studio. In
1924, I organized a handicraft workshop
and made models ordered by state
institutions and theaters: *Inga*, the
Theater of the Revolution; *Aelita*, for the
cinema; and the play *The Inspector
General*, MOSPS.
In 1925, at the request of the Kustexport
Corporation, I organized and executed
models for the Paris Exhibition, receiving
First Prize.
In 1926 I made designs for the peoples
of the North, commissioned by
Vsekopromsoiuz. In 1928, I designed for
the exhibition of Arts and Handicrafts of
the State Academy of Artistic Sciences.
In 1926, I made, after Golovin's sketches,
costumes for the play *The Marriage of
Figaro* at the Art Theater.
In 1929, I fulfilled an order for designs to
be exported. In 1930, I made fur models
for the exhibition in Leipzig,
commissioned by All-Union Western
Chamber of Commerce.
In 1929, on order from Vsekopromsoiuz,
I executed designs for the exhibition in
New York, and a year later worked as
chief of the design workshop of the Furs
Combine.
In 1932, I took employment at the Art
Theater as a consultant and constructor.
In cinematography, I made the costumes
for the films: *The Generation of Winners,
The Circus* (Lenfilm), *The Inspector
General* (Ukrfilm), and *Alexandr Nevsky*.

Moscow Art Academic Theater of the USSR
13 February 1933.

Arkhiv MKhAT, d. 5085/1-6. Copy.

Nadezhda Lamanova

Nadezhda Lamanova holds a special place among the clothes designers of the 1920s, not only because she was the first professional clothing designer of her time, but also because of the immense contribution she made to the development of theoretical principles of Soviet design, and the creation of the first examples of contemporary clothing.

Her professional life began in 1885, when, at the age of 24, she opened her own workshop. Her talent soon made itself known, and when she opened a business in Moscow she enjoyed great popularity and a wide clientele among intellectuals, writers, actors, and artists. What attracted everyone was not only Lamanova's exceptional talent and her professional skill, but a genuine artistic trustworthiness. Her keen eye, subtle taste, and thorough knowledge of costume helped her to immediately grasp the peculiarities of a person's character and figure and to decide unerringly on the most suitable cut and style of dress.

Annual trips to Paris, the fashion center of that time, refined her knowledge. She collaborated with France's most celebrated designer, Paul Poiret, who instantly recognized the Russian artist's extraordinary

82

talent and repeatedly asked her to move to Paris to work with him. Lamanova, however, refused.

On the eve of the October Revolution, when Lamanova was 46 years old, her firm claimed the uppermost aristocratic circles as its clients, and its signboard included the inscription "Provider to the Court of His Imperial Majesty."

Perhaps some artists in their declining years, who had earned official and public recognition and a firm position in society, might not have survived the spiritual upheaval of the revolution and its intrusion into their artistic lives. Lamanova, however, unhesitatingly embraced the revolution, and approved its ideals. She explained her position:

"The revolution has changed my property status, but it has not changed my fundamental ideas; in fact it has given me the opportunity to put them into practice on an incomparably larger scale."[27]

27.
Notes of N. Lamanova. Manuscript. Archives of T. Strizhenova.

Her position can be understood through her biography. Nadezhda Lamanova was the child of a serviceman of modest means, became an orphan while very young and had to support her younger sister, combining work with study. In the years of the First World War, when Lamanova was already solidly established, she readily allowed her estate to be used as a military hospital.

Kindness, humanitarianism, and simplicity were her principal characteristics. She parted with her firm and the privileges of her position without complaint. She also underwent many difficult experiences: she

85

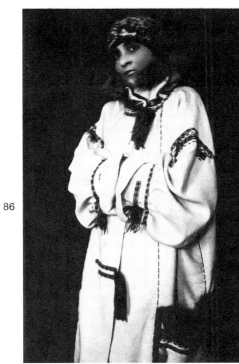

86

83-85

Lilia Brik and Alexandra
Khokhlova, a silent film star,
modelling Lamanova's designs in
1923. Cloche hats were
fashionable at that time.
Lamanova and her younger sister
Maria ornamented these hats with
old embroidery. One of
Lamanova's favorite clients and
models was Alexandra Khokhlova.
The designer emphasized the
eccentricity of her model's
manners and facial expression
with flashy garments of striped
fabrics. The dynamic rhythm of
the stripes in the blouse contrast
with the quiet lines of a narrow
black skirt.

86

A summer coat ornamented with
folk embroidery designed by
Lamanova. 1923.

87-90

Lamanova's designs of 1923-1925, a silk dress trimmed with fur. Sometimes an almost uncut shawl with a patterned border became the front of a costume. Lamanova had folk-embroidered towels inserted in the form of an apron into a chemise-type dress. Handmade embroidery formed an integral part of the construction of a garment. With her fine sense of form Lamanova could combine the detail of folk embroidery with an asymmetrical row of buttons, an item which could then be worn over the dress. 1923.

89

88

spent the first years after the Revolution in the Butyrskaia prison, indicted as a "bourgeoise," and was later released through the intercession of the writer Maxim Gorky, then head of the state publishing house. In the 1930s she was disfranchised, and she and her friends had to argue tirelessly to prove how much she had done for the Soviet system. No humiliation seemed to crush the will of this remarkable woman.

Lamanova's creative biography is also very complicated. Prior to the revolution, she worked in the fashionable *"moderne"* style, her productions following the trends in Paris garments. Several such dresses are in Leningrad's Hermitage Museum. Intended for the Russian aristocracy, they are characterized by an intricate and labor-intensive execution, and also by the use of expensive foreign fabrics and decoration. Although different from each other in cut, shape and decorative details, they are similar in the elegance of the silhouette, perfect proportion, and clever choice of the texture and color — in a word, they possess the harmony that distinguishes a work of art from ordinary tailoring.

90

The gift of Nadezhda Lamanova was not unlike a sculptor's talent — she could envision how each fabric would look on a person and what shape suited the figure. She herself did not make the garment, but did "the pinning" of the material on a human figure, delineating the contours of the cut and of the decoration. Her method of dress design could be called "sculpting in fabric."

Lamanova often told her students that the most important aspect of their work was finding the shape of costume that was appropriate to the person, not inventing a "style" or fashionable attributes that allegedly determine the aesthetic merits of clothes. She believed that costume was inseparable from the individual. Therefore the artist banished the words "style" and "fashion" from the designers' vocabulary, replacing them with the notions of "shape" and "design." She was the first to draw a line between the tasks of costume designer and seamstress, emphasizing their specificity:

"I create designs of women's clothes, I do the pinning and determine the shape and decoration, but I do not perform the technical part of the work. I cannot do this work as an architect cannot build a house, or as a blacksmith cannot work without a striker."[28] Lamanova did not make sketches of her designs, because she could not draw; they are known from photographs of the actual models housed in her personal archives.[29]

28.
Ibid.

29.
These archives were kindly presented to me by the artist's younger sister Maria Petrovna and her niece Nadezhda Krakht. Reminiscences of her relatives, students, and acquaintances, almost all of whom are now dead, are also important for understanding Lamanova's art. I was particularly helped in the preparation of this book by the now deceased F. Gorelenkova and N. Makarova, two of Nadezhda Lamanova's students.

Whereas in private life Nadezhda Lamanova was exceptionally kind, in her work she was severe and demanding, totally confident that her point of view was correct. She rarely took into account the clients' wishes and was firm in her choice of design. Fitting was for her a truly creative act: she pondered over the style and the system of cutting, considered the distribution of folds of the textile on the figure, bearing in mind all the particularities of construction in relation to the shape of the body. She paid attention, moreover, not only to the lines of the "front" but also to the figure as a plastic volume, always checking to see how the dress changed when it moved.

As the actors who knew Nadezhda Lamanova recalled, it was at once difficult and easy to work with her. It was difficult because of the way she tenaciously decided on the style of the costume, disregarding their wishes. She made long and repeated fittings, tiring the client, until she was sure that everything was perfect. On the other hand it was easy, because she was absolutely reliable: the result of the work was always an irreproachably made dress.

With the Revolution a new era began in Lamanova's life: her talent and immense practical experience allowed her at last to engage in large-scale and diverse activities. Taking the lead in restructuring garment production, the artist experienced in her later years a rejuvenation of her

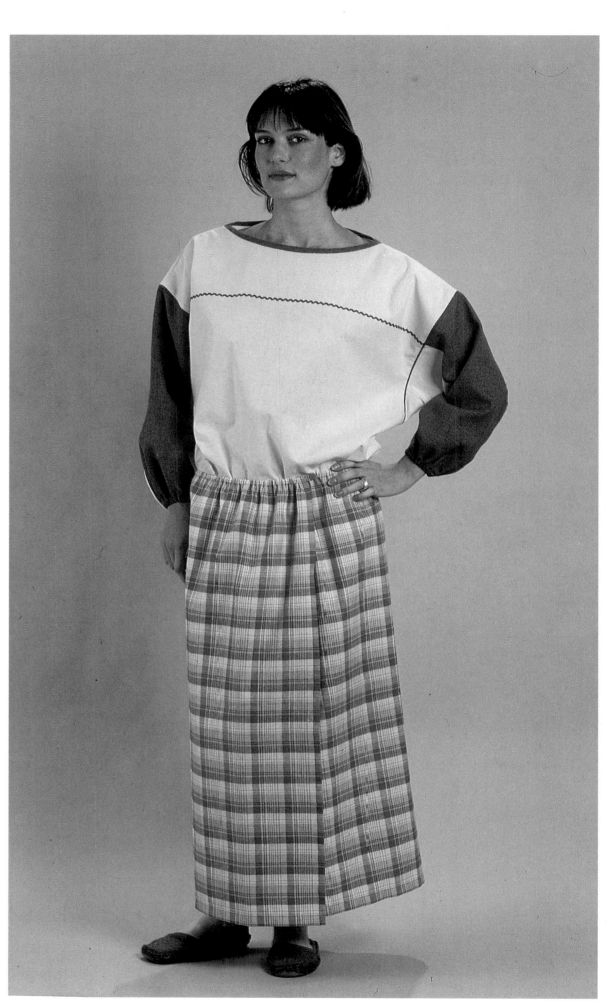

91
Lilia Brik modelling Lamanova's
dress made of homespun textiles.
1923.

92
The same dress reconstructed
in 1985 by Elena Khudiakova.
Khudiakova, a well-known
designer in her own right,
models the dress.

93, 94
Lamanova's designs of 1923.
Costumes made of unbleached
linen and a coarse wool cloth
typified textiles of the austere
years.

creative powers. She joined the work of Soviet institutions with enthusiasm, showing outstanding organizational abilities. She created the Workshops of Contemporary Dress at the Narkompros industrial art subsection, became a member of the dress section of the State Academy of Artistic Sciences, and collaborated on the journals *Atelier* and *Krasnaia niva*, both as the author of articles and as clothing designer. The concept of the purpose of art expressed in the romantic revolutionary slogans of those turbulent days, and the desire to integrate art into all aspects of daily life and industry, stuck a responsive chord in the designer.

Despite her time-consuming administrative and organizational work, she continued to design clothes. She wrote in 1922: "My work consists of creating designs of modern women's clothes, and I have always tried to use simplicity and logic in my designs, proceeding usually from the specific characteristics of the fabric. . . ."[30]

30.
TsGALI, f. 941, op. 10, d. 341, p. 3.

93

In the years following the revolution, Lamanova had a clear conception of the trends in Soviet costume: clothes for everyday wear and clothes featuring folk motifs. For models, Lamanova most often used Alexandra Khokhlova, a silent-film actress, her student Nadezhda Makarova, and Lilia Brik. Sometimes the amateur photographs taken of these clothes are joined to a narrow swatch of the textile from which the garment was made. They are plain, poorly colored and, as a rule, non-patterned textiles: brown Holland, flannelette and calico. With them the artist produced simple dresses of elongated proportions, mostly of the chemise type. For ornament, use was sometimes made of decorative colored insets, or the alternating of dark stripes on a white ground, which somewhat resembled the con-

structivists' geometric drawings; often a subtle pattern of the fabic was the basis for the decoration of the dress. One feels that Lamanova deliberately, and on principle, tried to simplify the cut. In her explanatory note to the Workshops of Contemporary Dress, the artist pointed out that the new workshops could develop "methods for simplifying costume as a characteristic feature of worker's garments in contrast to the garments of the bourgeoisie."[31] But that was not her only motive for simplicity.

31.
N. Lamanova's personal archives.

Unpretentious clothes were certainly suited to the austere life of that time. What were needed were garments that were simple, comfortable, inexpensive and practical. The available materials — limp fabrics that could not keep their shape or, on the other hand, thick, coarse material (mostly soldiers' cloth) — dictated the form the garment would take. No wonder Lamanova's basic formula was: "Material determines the shape."

The amateur photographs in her archives allow us to follow the current of her artistic search. For instance, one can see three models of

a coat very similar in cut: they have in common a straight silhouette, a stand-up collar and a wide belt.

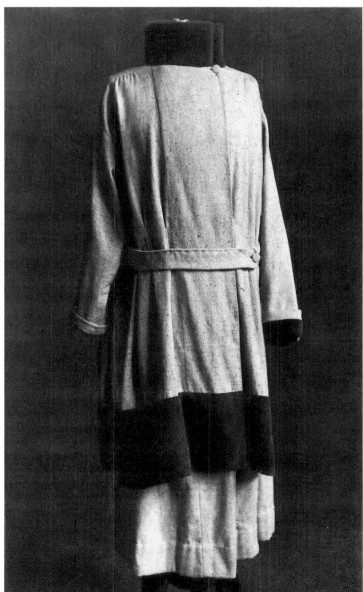

But each model has its own solution, depending on its purpose. In the short coat of woollen cloth, stress is laid on the streamlined statuesque form, with its sections made conspicuous by raised stitching. Beside it is a model of the same coat made of canvas, a thinner material: it has tucks under the stand-up collar producing a picturesque play of rigid little pleats; the belt is clasped with a buckle wrapped with string; it has below, in the middle, a rectangular cut-out that gives the garment originality and performs a definite function—preventing creases when walking. In the third version of the

95

96

95
Lamanova's designs of 1925.
A coat.

96
Lilia Brik in Lamanova's two-color
costume. 1923.

coat (probably made of flannelette), proportions are altered: it is longer and considerably wider than the first two, hence the fabric falls in soft folds. The waist is tightly girdled with a wide sash. Lamanova thus demonstrated the possibilities of offering several versions from a single construction.

Lamanova's archives contain one watercolor sketch, which depicts an unusual model of a dress in varying tones of blue. It is not signed, but, judging by the subtle color scheme and the sure and free stroke of the brush, the executor could have been Lamanova's friend Alexandra Exter. This dress, too, is cut as a chemise, with a high neck, rather wide sleeves and a wide twice-wound sash of the same material linked with a decorative black buckle in a convex rectangle. Worn over the dress is a short jacket with sleeves shorter and wider than those of the dress. This deceptively simple model is a masterpiece. This detail forms a second version of the attire. The modest, refined ornamental details include strips of grey, terra-cotta, and blue decorating the collar, cuffs and sash. This deceptively simple model is a masterpiece. It was to be made of a fabric like crepe satin and was therefore to serve as a "fancy" dress. It is likely, however, that the garment was never made. Lamanova also designed a large series of everyday dresses made from a single shape, an elongated rectangle. These simple garments acquired individuality because of the decorative appliqué in the form of broken geometric lines or of thin semicircles.

Lamanova exhibited much more freedom when designing dresses displaying folk motifs. Her treatment of these motifs was absolutely extemporaneous and always surprising. She would use pieces of genuine antique lace for the bottom of a dress with a modern picot edging, employ a genuine Russian towel for the front of the dress, and make the bodices from lace curtains richly embroidered in satin-stitch. This was not mere "appliqué," as in many such works of folk art, but the design of an integral construction as a plastic volume, a coordination of all its elements. This side of Lamanova's work was quite deliberate: she was well aware that she addressed amateur dressmakers, who, by using her methods, could improve their garments and individualize them with folk-embroidered towels, pillow-covers, crochet-work and other traditional household fabrics.

It was a garment of this genre that the artist sent to the Exposition internationale des arts décoratifs et industriels modernes held in Paris in 1925. The rectangular-shaped dress included a richly embroidered towel in its lower section; similar towels were used for the sides and the back. A narrow red braid edged the neckline and sleeves, harmonizing the whole. There was a modish little hat to match. This ensemble, simple but sensational, produced quite a stir among the sophisticated Paris public. Lamanova received the Grand Prix "for national originality combined with the modern fashion trend." In her article "The Russian Style," Lamanova wrote: "One of the interesting endeavors in the field of modern costume is the modification of the forms and character of folk costumes and their application to everyday clothing. The rationality of the folk costume, thanks to the age-old collective efforts of the people, can serve both as the ideological and the practical model for our urban clothes. The basic forms of folk costume are always wise. . . . It is by introducing specific colors and distributing them in rhythmic succession on a rationally made costume that we make the type of clothes that are in harmony with our contemporary life." [32]

32.
Krasnaya niva, 1923, no. 30, p. 32. Though the article is not signed, most people agree that it was very likely written by Lamanova. Moreover, a sample of a garment illustrating it closely resembles the sketches found in the artist's personal archives and in her article "On the Contemporary Costume," published in the journal *Krasnaia niva* (1927, no. 27, pp. 662-663).

Sometimes the designer incorporated seemingly discordant elements: in a fashionable "mantelet-dress," for example, she used a fragment of folk embroidery, strips of different color along the hemline and the cuffs, and a long row of large buttons asymmetrically placed along the side. The unusual mantelet began at the sleeves and formed part of a kerchief that hung in a triangle down the back. The mantelet could be worn over an everyday dress, transforming it into an original, fashionable ensemble.

The artist's favorite type of clothing was a woman's suit comprising a dress, a skirt, and a jacket that she called a "caftan." These ensembles could highlight the quality of the fabric (when it was of good quality) and, of equal importance, allow the designer to compare and contrast the parts: a narrow straight skirt with a loose-fitting blouse; a straight

97

98

97, 98
Lamanova's designs of 1923.
A costume incorporating
embroidered towels. Using
available materials — a curtain or
a coverlet — Lamanova
constructed a fashionable garment
in white tulle with a lace fringe.
The ensemble consists of a long
straight blouse, a straight skirt, a
small hat and a belt ornamented
with similar decorative elements.

long dress with extra-wide sleeves; sometimes a dress draped with asymmetrically placed pleats. Lamanova believed that contrast in the design
of models made them dynamic: "The absence of contrast and, consequently, of dynamism makes the silhouette dry, monotonous, and lifeless."

Both Lamanova's theories and practice closely resembled constructivism in their functionalism and expediency. In the artist's works, however,
the image-bearing, emotional principle always predominates. Ornament
and color were its vehicles. Lamanova's theory on the laws of ornamentation of clothes is also very interesting, although not directly related to
design for mass production. In her best works the artist displayed a sense
of proportion in the nature and placement of the garment's finishing
touch, the ornament. Unprinted fabrics and the straight chemise-type
silhouettes left large plain surfaces requiring decoration. Following folk
principles of ornamentation, Lamanova distributed decorative elements
in places dictated by the garment's construction, such as the bodice,

101

99
Lamanova's designs of 1923.
Costumes trimmed with lace and
embroidery.

100, 101
A Lamanova design from 1923.
A dress decorated with braid.

102, 103
Clothes by Nadezhda Lamanova,
Alexandra Exter, and Evgenia
Pribylskaia shown at the exhibition
of modern woman's costume in
Moscow in 1923. On display were
mostly richly ornamented dresses
made of homespun fabrics with
embroidery based on the
principles of folk costume.

shoulders, cuffs, and hem. Most often she used genuine folk motifs — the borders of napkins or towels — but sometimes she herself made the ornament in a constructivist or modern style. The peculiarities and rhythm of the decoration harmonized with the overall outline, the specific cut, the texture and color of the fabric. Ornament in everyday costume became Lamanova's preoccupation after 1924, when she was made head of the arts and crafts workshop that filled orders for Kustexport (Handicrafts Export) and other organizations for domestic and international exhibitions. The designer began to pay more attention to ethnicity in costume and decoration. Captivated by the decorative splendor of embroidery, she occasionally used it to excess, and these designs seemed less integrated than her more restrained models.

It is easy to see from her archives that all the works of Nadezhda Lamanova, however varied they might seem, have in common "a single foundation," the rectangle. Taking into consideration the properties and possibilities of the fabrics that were available, the artist "translated" the rectangle into countless clothing designs. The starting point for most dressmakers was fashion; they disregarded the properties of the material, and even tried to disguise them with elaborate decorative design. Neither the individual characteristics nor even the figure of the wearer had much bearing on the design. No wonder the corset lasted so long (in Europe it was still being worn in the 1920s). This artificial frame altered and often distorted the figure, subordinating it to the construction of the dress.

104

104

N. Lamanova. Sketch of a costume. 1923. (The sketch is by A. Exter.)

105

A graphic scheme of a cut by N. Lamanova. 1923.

106-109

Title page and pages from the album *Iskusstvo v bytu* (Art in Everyday Life). 1925. Nadezhda Lamanova was fascinated by the idea of creating clothing for the masses. She believed that art must embrace all spheres of everyday life. With her close friend Vera Mukhina, one of the outstanding sculptors of 20th-century Russia, Lamanova produced in 1925 the album *Iskusstvo v bytu*. Drawings in the album were by Mukhina and the painter V. Akhmetiev.

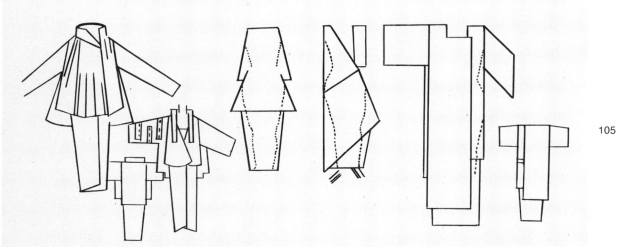

105

In Lamanova's designs the figure was not subordinated to the material; in fact the opposite was true. It is the figure that prompts what fabric to use, just as the figure determines the color. Inelastic, stiff fabrics worked best with the simple form of a rectangle. Lamanova's use of this form did not clash with the most up-to-date trends in European fashion at that time. European clothes had the same outline, elongated proportions and accentuated vertical lines. The Russian artist's designs appeared similar but at the same time they were fundamentally different — they were simpler, more practical, and met everyday requirements. In the "chemise" style, again based on the rectangle, Lamanova was attracted by its simple cut, its inexpensiveness, and the almost complete absence of leftover material after cutting (which is important when textiles are scarce). But, even more significant, these clothes could in theory be quickly and easily mass-produced on the factory conveyor belt, even with the unsophisticated garment manufacturing processes of those years. Combining art with industrial production was one of Lamanova's lifelong goals. In the first item of the program for the Workshops of Contemporary Dress she wrote: "to introduce elements of artistry into the manufacture of dress." The backward state of the industry, however, did not allow

Lamanova's projects to reach fruition, and she was compelled to remain within the limits of laboratory experiments.

Frustrated with the lack of industrial capacity to provide the population with decent modern clothing, Lamanova tried to enlist still another category of the population. With her closest friend Vera Mukhina, she published in 1925 the album *Iskusstvo v bytu* (Art in Everyday Life), in which they addressed women who made their own dresses, offering them their designs of everyday clothes, which were simple in cut and easy to understand even for beginners. Each drawing of a model was accompanied by its pattern and a detailed description of appropriate fabrics, and even color suggestions. In geometrizing their drawings, the authors simplified their patterns to the extreme, while subscribing to the tenets of the well-known constructivists, who divided all drawings into geometric planes. The editorial in the album said that the condition of the country at the time "does not provide sufficient material prerequisites for a radical transformation of our entire culture, which will come with the final triumph of socialism. . . . The new forms, the culture of dressing, the rational and well - arranged everyday life . . . can be achieved without the aid of professionals, but with the creative efforts of the working

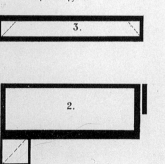

108

109

The distinguishing feature of the designs is their simplicity and functionality of cut. The authors addressed their journal to self-taught dressmakers. The title page says that the album contains 36 tables within the sections Toys, Clothes, Village Library and Reading-Room, Club and Theater. Homespun linen could be used to make a Young Pioneer uniform for boys and girls. The album includes samples of banners, which are designed in a spirit of constructivism, without the "fringe, tassels and other unnecessary details." The black banner is a "banner of permanent mourning." It has the inscription: "Fighters die, the Revolution lives on." Lamanova advises using durable linen fabrics to make a comfortable sports outfit including a blouse and a skirt or trousers. Patterns and explanations are given next to the drawings.

33.
Iskusstvo v bytu. Moscow, 1925.

family, of the school or club collective."[33] Lamanova was continually aware — whether she designed for the industry or for a small workshop — of the possibility of her patterns being used at home. Her models encouraged amateur dressmakers to seek simple, expedient forms, and taught them a judicious use of folk themes.

The album displayed summer and winter dresses, jackets and coats, sports clothes and a "Young Pioneer" uniform. There were even theater costumes by Vladimir Akhmetiev, including the costume of a female worker, which could be easily transformed into the costume of a "bourgeoise." Both the cut and decorative elements of the designs emphasized their distinctive national character. One of the most interesting samples was a dress made of kerchiefs. The cashmere fabric and the small red and green flowers printed on the kerchief gave the native-looking costume a fashionable appeal. Also attractive was a costume in three versions: to be worn in the street, at home, and at work. Its transformations depended on minimal alterations. A straight, impressive-looking coat was cut, with utmost simplicity, from a length of army cloth. It is described in the album: "The coat (the width of the fabric being about two meters) is of one piece. Only the arm-hole is cut out. The sleeve has only one seam: the projecting piece in the pattern, when folded in two, forms a gusset for free arm movement. The collar represents half a square; its long diagonal side is sewn beneath the neck following the dotted line. After being sewn on, the remaining ends of the collar are buttoned on the shoulder line. If the cloth is narrower, the sides have

34.
Iskusstvo v bytu. Moscow, 1925 (from the description of the model).

seams, with the form of the rectangle remaining."[34] The garments in the album include a sort of *prozodezhda*: a Tolstoy-style man's shirt, a blouse and a skirt (designer V. Akhmetiev); a sports outfit consisting of a blouse and culottes; and headgear (designer V. Mukhina). The album also contains easy-to-execute building projects: a village library and reading-room, a village theater, a bookcase combined with a show-case, and much more. Artists from different fields tried to assist in creating, with minimal resources, a new environment appropriate to the new life. The design of the album, by Vera Mukhina, was well conceived and

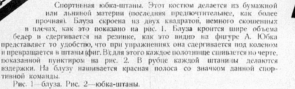

СПОРТИВНЫЙ КОСТЮМ

Спортивная юбка-штаны. Этот костюм делается из бумажной или льняной материи (последняя предпочтительнее, как более прочная). Блуза скроена из двух квадратов, немного скошенных в плечах, как это показано на рис. 1. Блуза кроится шире объема бедер и сдергивается на резинке, как это видно на фигуре А. Юбка представляет то удобство, что при упражнениях она сдергивается под коленом и превращается в штаны фиг. В; для этого каждое полотнище сшивается по черте, показанной пунктиром на рис. 2. В рубце каждой штанины делаются вздержки. На блузу нашивается красная полоса со значком данной спортивной команды.

Рис. 1—блуза. Рис. 2—юбка-штаны.

110

ДОМАШНЕЕ ПЛАТЬЕ из ГОЛОВНОГО ПЛАТКА

В этом платье за основу взят квадрат головного кашемирового платка, и поэтому весь план его построен на квадрате. Добавочная черная материя—такой же кашемир, как и платок. Требуется ее 3½ до 4 метров. Зеленые полосы сделаны из легкой шелковой материи; можно делать их и из шерстяной. Излишнюю ширину кафтана в бедрах надо заколоть в складку с левой стороны или опоясать узким черным кушаком (отнюдь не над талией).

На рисунке 1—пунктиром обозначена форма нижней рубахи, верхнюю часть которой можно делать из более легкой материи. Для более худой фигуры рукав можно делать приблизительно на ладонь уже и ставить ластовицу зеленого цвета. Один рукав показан нами в плане, другой—сшитый.

Это платье можно делать также из бумажной материи с применением бумажных головных платков.

111

110, 111

Pages from the album *Iskusstvo v bytu*, 1925. Designs by N. Lamanova. Lamanova suggests using woollen or cotton kerchiefs to make a house dress. The cut is based on a square. Lamanova explains how the pattern should be altered for a more slender figure. A summer dress can be made of brown Holland cloth. The pattern shows two versions of the design, with and without sleeves. The dress is trimmed with a fabric dyed at home in a contrasting color.

Пальто (при ширине ткани около 2-х метров) делается без швов из одного полотнища. Прорезы делаются только для проймы. Рукав с одним швом; выступающий кусок на выкройке, будучи сложен пополам, образует ластовицу для свободы движения руки. Воротник (рис. 2) образует половину квадрата, широкой стороной по косой нитке, пришивается ниже выреза ворота по пунктиру (показанному на рис. 1). После пришивки оставшиеся концы ворота застегиваются на линии плеча на пуговицы. Если ткань уже — делаются швы на боках с сохранением формы прямоугольника.
Рис. 1—общий план пальто. Рис. 2 — воротник. Рис. 3—

112

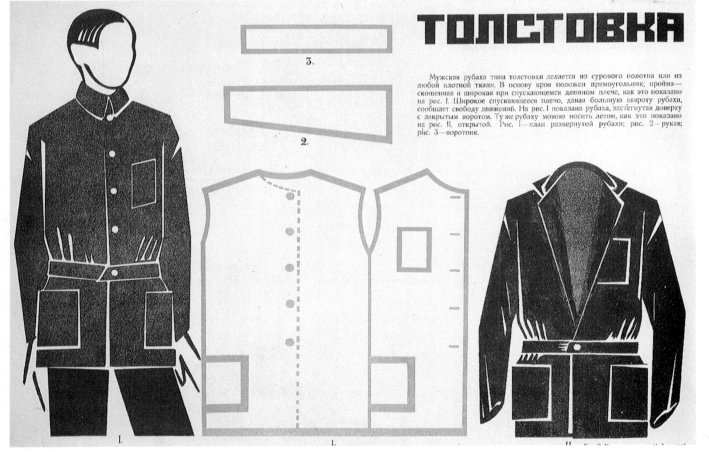

ТОЛСТОВКА

Мужская рубаха типа толстовки делается из сурового полотна или из любой плотной ткани. В основу кроя положен прямоугольник; пройма—скошенная и широкая при спускающемся длинном плече, как это показано на рис. I. Широкое спускающееся плечо, давая большую широту рубахи, сообщает свободу движений. На рис. I показана рубаха, застегнутая доверху с закрытым воротом. Ту же рубаху можно носить летом, как это показано на рис. II, открытой. Рис. I—план развернутой рубахи; рис. 2—рукав; рис. 3—воротник.

113

112, 113

Pages from the album *Iskusstvo v bytu*, 1925. Designs by Lamanova, including the so-called Tolstoy-style shirt and a coat made of army cloth. Loose linen blouses were very popular among Russian intellectuals who imitated Leo Tolstoy's style of dress. While retaining the name of the shirt, Lamanova altered the cut. In her interpretation the shirt is close to the constructivists' *prozodezhda* and barely resembles the loose half-peasant shirts with a yoke. The cut of the coat is quite original, with no seams at the sides and with a triangular collar.

splendidly executed down to the smallest detail. The combination of original drawings and plans, handsome typography and skillful use of color made the volume an illustrious example of fine art in design.

Lamanova worked on everyday costume design approximately until the mid-1920s, and for some time after that was occupied with the design of models from homespun textiles. Her contribution to the theory of garment design was substantial. She wrote the program for the Workshops of Contemporary Dress and the curricula of the first Soviet schools for clothing design, made reports at conferences and wrote a number of articles for the journal *Krasnaia niva*. It appears that the artist was preparing to publish a book summing up her extensive experience. She wrote in 1922 in her autobiography: "I have started to organize the data that I have worked out and put to practical use during my career."[35]

35.
GAKhN, f. 941, op. 1, d. 341. Autobiography of N. Lamanova.

Even if Lamanova could not draw, she certainly had a writer's gift. Her many articles impress not only by their splendid mastery of the intricate problems of costume, but also by their logic and compositional harmony and their original turn of phrase. In her article "The Russian Style," Lamanova raised the question of the new Soviet costume and tradition.[36] Her well-known article "On Contemporary Costume"[37] contains a classification of the new forms of clothes into everyday and holiday attire, shows their kinship to the principles of folk costume, and analyzes in detail the necessity of constructing a costume to suit the individual figure.

36.
Krasnaia niva, 1923, no. 30, p. 32.

37.
Krasnaia niva, 1924, no. 27, pp. 662-663.

Lamanova's writings include another article prepared for the press, "On the Rationality of Costume." It apparently served as the basis for the 1928 theoretical program. It was here that the artist formulated the "principal factors of costume," and gave her famous maxim, "the purpose for which the costume is created, for whom and from what," which she advanced as the creed of clothing designers.

Lamanova's theory was made public in full in 1928 and was presented at the exhibition of Handmade Textiles and Embroidery in Woman's Contemporary Costume. The main items of the program were the costume's purpose, its material, the figure of its wearer, and its form:

КАФТАН ИЗ 2х ВЛАДИМИРЕСКИХ ПОЛОТЕНЕЦ

Кафтан сделан из двух холщевых кустарных полотенец: юбка сделана или из такого же холста, или из какой-либо другой материи синего или черного цвета. Кафтан определяется шириной полотенец. Боковые полотнища сдернуты на резинку на высоте бедер или немного ниже (в зависимости от фигуры), но только отнюдь не над талией, чтобы не нарушалась форма прямоугольника. Естественная ширина полотенца спадает с плеча наподобие короткого рукава. Эту же форму можно делать и из другой ткани — бумажной или шерстяной: в этом случае вышивка заменяется полосатой материей. Рис. 1—развернутый план кафтана. Рис. 2—спина.

Рис. В. Мухина по модели Н. Л...

114

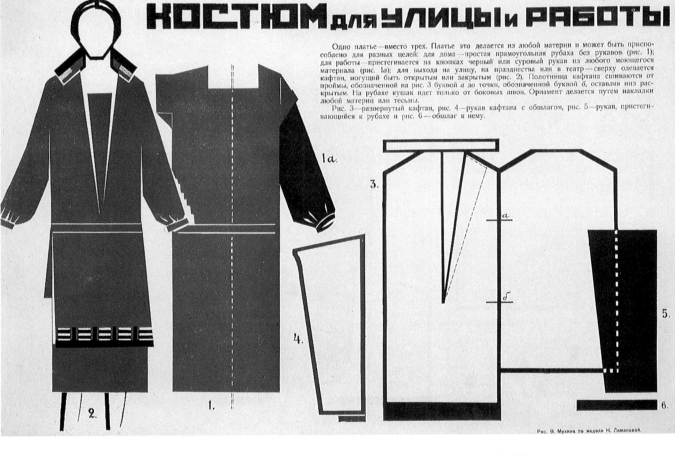

КОСТЮМ для УЛИЦЫ и РАБОТЫ

Одно платье—вместо трех. Платье это делается из любой материи и может быть приспособлено для разных целей: для дома—простая прямоугольная рубаха без рукавов (рис. 1); для работы—пристегивается на кнопках черный или суровый рукав из любого моющегося материала (рис. 1a); для выхода на улицу, на празднества или в театр—сверху одевается кафтан, могущий быть открытым или закрытым (рис. 2). Полотнища кафтана сшиваются от проймы, обозначенной на рис. 3 буквой a до точки, обозначенной буквой б, оставляя низ раскрытым. На рубахе кушак идет только от боковых швов. Орнамент делается путем накладки любой материи или тесьмы.

Рис. 3—развернутый кафтан, рис. 4—рукав кафтана с обшлагом, рис. 5—рукав, пристегивающийся к рубахе и рис. 6—обшлаг к нему.

Рис. В. Мухина по модели Н. Ламановой.

115

114, 115

Pages from the album *Iskusstvo v bytu*, 1925. Designs by Lamanova. A caftan made of two towels from the Vladimir region and a costume for wear on the street and at work. The 1920s saw an acute shortage of textiles, which was why Lamanova designed clothes to be made of kerchiefs, army cloth (there were no other woollens) and embroidered towels. Necessity is, indeed, the mother of invention.

The costume's purpose determines the material.

The material determines the form.

The figure, in turn, determines the material and color.

The form determines the material, the ornament, and the rhythm that coordinates these elements.

Ornament is used to integrate the material and the color.

Ornament is used to construct both the form and the weight.

Ornament divides the plane both artistically and constructively.

The form of the rectangle is determined by the material.

Material should be used sparingly, with little waste in construction. The form should permit free movement.[38]

38.
From T. Armand, *Ornamentastia tkani*. Moscow, Leningrad, Akadenmia, 1931. p. 103.

These brief theses, which today might seem self-evident, caused a revolution in the art of dress. They created the foundation for a vast branch of decorative art which was in keeping with the nature of the new life, and was also its product. The principles of Lamanova's theory can still be applied today, not only in costume design, but in other decorative arts.

Another important sphere of the remarkable artist's activities was her work for theater and cinema. Lamanova was employed by the Moscow Art Theater for forty years, from 1901 to 1941, the year of her death. She created a multitude of costumes, for foreign classics as well as for plays by Soviet authors. The artist's gift in this field was described by Stanislavsky in his letter to Alexandr Golovin, the designer of scenery and costumes for the 1926 performance at the Art Theater of Beaumarchais's comedy, "The Marriage of Figaro": "We attempted having costumes made in the rough by ordinary tailors and dressmakers. The attempt proved beyond doubt that these people will not be able to convey the enormity of your talent. Nothing else was left to us but to apply to the person whom we consider to be the only one in Moscow artistically sensitive enough to materialize your sketches. This person is Lamanova. Perhaps you think that she is just another dressmaker who makes contemporary costume fashionable, but in fact Lamanova is a great artist, who, when she saw your sketches, responded with a true artistic ardor.

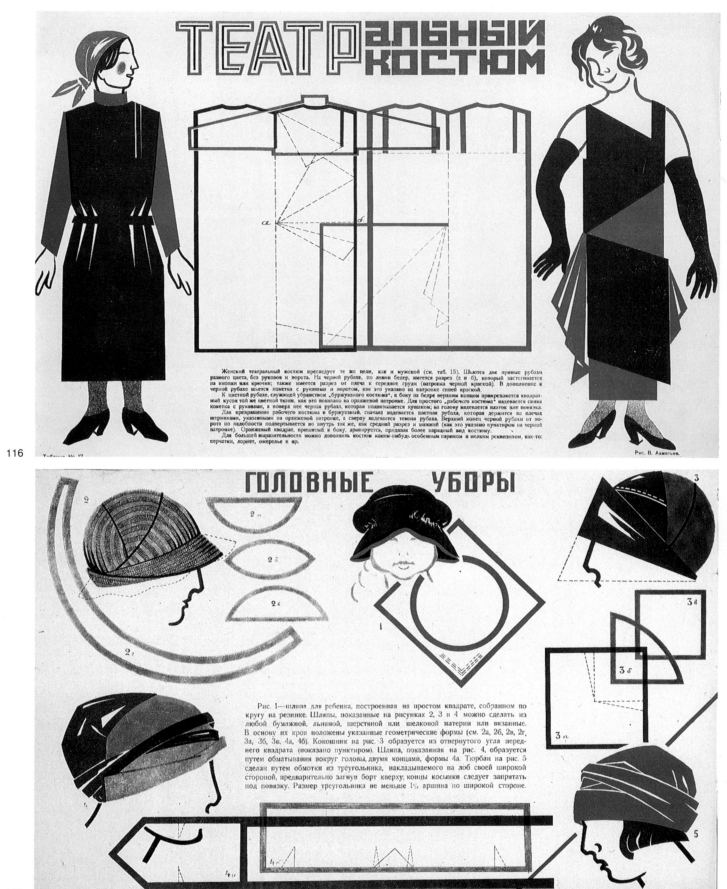

116

116, 117

Pages from the album *Iskusstvo v bytu*, 1925. A theatrical costume by the artist Vladimir Akhmetiev. The explanatory notes show how two costumes — ''working-class'' and ''bourgeois'' — can be made from one pattern. Headgear after V. Mukhina's sketches. While helping Lamanova to sketch her ideas, Mukhina designed clothes independently as well. Her headgear balances between the proletarian kerchief and hats of the Art Deco style.

39.
K. Stanislavsky. *Sobranie sochinenii*, vol. 8. Moscow, Iskusstvo Publishers, 1961. pp. 136-137.

For each costume she will be seeking with her own hands not hackneyed nor trite but highly individual methods of tailoring."[39] In the 1920s, Nadezhda Lamanova also became involved with the Evgeni Vakhtangov Theater, the Revolution Theater, and the Red Army Theater. In her work for the cinema, she made the costumes for the films *Aelita* (directed by Yakov Protazanov), *Ivan the Terrible*, *Alexandr Nevsky* (directed by Sergei Eisenstein), *The Generation of Winners*, *The Circus* (directed by Grigorii Alexandrov), and others.

Soviet Costume at the 1925 International Exhibition of Decorative and Industrial Arts in Paris

The attempt to create a new costume attracted many well-known artists hitherto engaged in other activities. In the early 1920s, Lamanova gathered together a group of talented enthusiasts: Vera Mukhina, by then a celebrated sculptor; Alexandra Exter, a talented painter and stage designer; Evgenia Pribylskaia, a connoisseur and prominent specialist in folk embroidery; and Nadezhda Makarova (Lamanova's niece), who was making her first steps in the design of a new costume under Lamanova's guidance in her workshop. Despite their differences of character and style, all of them accepted Lamanova's principles of creative dress design.

In 1925, Lamanova, Mukhina, Pribylskaia and Makarova were invited to take part in the preparation of the Soviet display at the International Exhibition of Decorative and Industrial Arts in Paris.[40] Their first task was to define the nature of models for the exhibition. There was no divergence in this respect: "Immediately all agreed . . . to invest all modern

40.
The exhibit of the Soviet section (architect K. Melnikov) included the interiors of a Workers' Club (A. Rodchenko) and of a village library and reading room (a group of designers). Books, textiles, crockery, and carpets were sold at the exhibition. The exhibits were awarded nine Grand Prix, 50 gold and 45 silver medals, and 30 honorary diplomas. *Moscow-Paris*, vol.1. Moscow, Sovetsky Khudozhnik Publishers, 1981. p. 77.

118

119
120

118
V. Mukhina. Sketch of a fashionable dress. 1923. Owing to its complex, somewhat "timeless" form, especially the draped full skirt and the striking hat, the outfit impresses by its rich imagination and beauty.

119, 120
Anonymous artist. Sketches of fashionable dresses reproduced in the review *Krasnaia niva* (Red Fields), 1923. Sporting a rather mannish collar, the straight dress of thick black and white silk is decorated with refined appliqué. The evening dress of crêpe de chine with a skirt of complicated cut is embroidered in beads. Both garments, of Art Deco style, are obviously borrowed from Western magazines. When compared with these, Vera Mukhina's originality is particularly evident, although her gift as a clothes designer did not fully reveal itself. Too busy as a sculptor, she could not devote much time to clothes design.

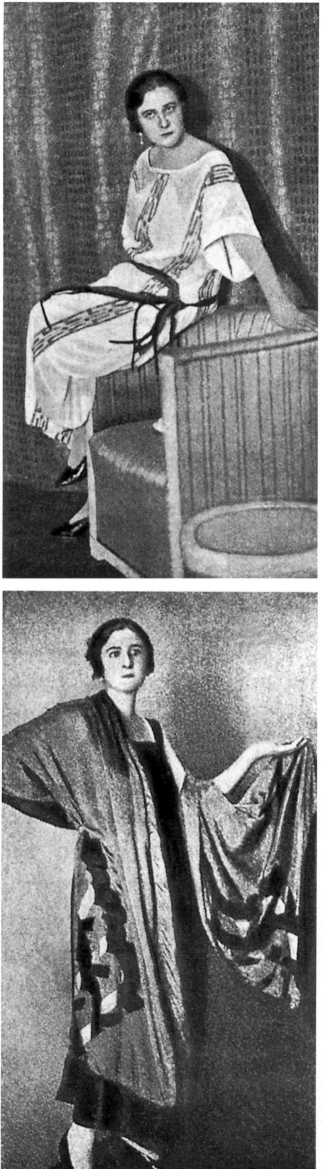

121

Evgeniia Pribylskaia (1878-1949)

Evgeniia Ivanovna Pribylskaia graduated from the school of painting in Kiev. In 1906 she abandoned painting to conduct research and work in the field of folk art. In 1910-1922, she headed the carpet-making and embroidery workshops in the Ukraine, collected samples of folk art and designed for the workshops.

After 1922 Pribylskaia lived in Moscow and participated in the revival and popularization of folk art. Her activities were connected in the 1920s with N. Lamanova's Workshops of Contemporary Dress, with Koverkusteksport (Carpet Export Organization) and the handicrafts section of the State Academy of Artistic Sciences; in the 1930s and the 1940s she was employed as a costume consultant at the Scientific Research Institute of Art Industry.

123

121-123

Designs by Evgeniia Pribylskaia, Lamanova's colleague and assistant in many undertakings. 1923. A prominent expert in folk weaving and embroidery, Pribylskaia did not copy elements of folk clothes or engage in compilation. The chemise-style dress is decorated with ornamental inserts. The simple black sleeveless dress is converted into an evening toilette with the help of draped silk shawls with geometric ornament.

124

E. Pribylsakaia. Ensemble of a chemise-style dress with embroidery and a shawl of transparent silk. 1923.

122

41.
Notes of N. Makarova.
Manuscript, Archives of
T. Strizhenova.

garments with our own national character, and this principle we made the foundation of our work.''[41]

Difficulties cropped up immediately; the artists needed materials, trimmings and decoration. Imagination and inventiveness came to their aid. It was decided to make dresses of a straight chemise shape from simple ''Russian'' fabrics: canvas, linen, and cotton. They were ornamented with decorative embroidered insets, either genuine folk embroidery or fashioned after Vera Mukhina's drawings. Mukhina herself prepared embroidery in an original and fashionable constructivist style, intricately weaving dynamic geometric compositions of vivid colors.

Each dress or costume had specially chosen headgear, handbags, and decoration that stylistically matched the garments. They featured some unusual materials: handbags of straw, string, cord, embroidered canvas; beads of wood, pebble, even breadcrumbs. Nikolai Bartran, chief of the handicrafts section of the State Academy of Artistic Sciences, helped design the accessories. Buttons and beads were polished with the help of lathes in his workshop, then painted with bright decorative patterns and varnished.

The inimitably original clothing ensembles were distinguished by a revived Russian folk tradition combined with 1920s fashion, and by impeccable taste and a high professional quality. Their success at the international exhibition was tremendous — the collection received the highest award for ''costume based on folk art.'' Through this exhibit the names of these Soviet designers became known abroad.

Besides the central figure of the group, Lamanova, special mention should be made of Vera Mukhina — her talent also proved itself to be brilliant and inimitable in this sphere of creative efforts. The two were not only colleagues, but bound by a close friendship. The creative legacy of Mukhina, one of the most important sculptors working in the Soviet Union during the 1920s, has been thoroughly studied, and her work in stage design and glassmaking is also relatively well known, but researchers have completely overlooked her contribution to everyday clothes design. In the 1920 and 1930s, however, Mukhina's activities in this field were extensive. She took an active part in the same organizations as

Lamanova: the Workshops of Contemporary Dress, the Atelier of Fashions, and the costume section of the State Academy of Artistic Sciences; her dress designs were published in the journal *Krasnaia niva* in the 1920s. In 1933, when the Moscow House of Clothing Design opened, Mukhina became a member of its Art Council. She started to work on everyday clothes models, no doubt under the influence of Lamanova — the two were inseparable, and in summer they lived together in Mukhina's cottage near Moscow. Costume design aroused Mukhina's interest not only by its unlimited artistic possibilities but also as an important branch of production closely connected with the life of the people, where artists' efforts and aspirations could be translated into reality. Moreover, the creation of a costume merged, in certain respects, with the art of sculpture. One can see how attentive the artist was to the "clothes" of her sculptured models. The splendidly arranged rhythms of the drapery and the folds of cloth in her sculptures often formed the decorative foundation of her clothing designs, and created some wonderfully expressive silhouettes.

Mukhina regarded the form of a dress as the core of construction. In her opinion, "when a pattern is being made, it is necessary to take care that the person in the garment be attractive from all sides, like a sculpture in the round, and not like a bas-relief that has come out of the wall with only the front shaped; that the person should be pleasant to look at from all points of view."[42] We could thus call "sculpturally perfect" her model of a dress shown in the magazine *Atelier*, although from a practical point of view it appears non-functional. It is a design that is noteworthy because in its characteristic volume, the flowing rhythms of its folds and the delicate pinkish-blue tones, it foretells the shapes of Mukhina's future works in glass. As a matter of fact, the famous Aster vase of thick smoky glass created by Mukhina in 1940, which had no analogy for its form or "image" in either domestic or foreign art glass of those years, obviously repeats by its bud-shaped form, its compositional rhythm, and its deep segmented facets the fashionable garment of 1923. In her approach to clothes design, Mukhina also reveals the style of an artist who understood and could apply the laws of theater costume.

42.
N. Makarova, "Vospominaniia o khudozhnike i druge." *Dekorativnoie iskusstvo SSSR*, 1958, no. 8, p. 12.

She did not merely depict a costume but also created the image of a woman elegant and full of grace, and seems to have been able to convey even the gait of her model.

When designing the journal *Iskusstvo v bytu*, Vera Mukhina not only brilliantly translated Lamanova's projects into drawings but also ventured to show her own headgear designs. These consisted of a variety of hats and specially cut triangular headscarves, very simple to make, judging by the concise patterns. Like Lamanova, the author based her versions of these hats and headscarves on one constructive foundation and a geometrized pattern.

From 1923 to 1926, Mukhina was active in designing new textiles, motivated by the need to set in motion a living art that could truly affect the life of the people. Her works were displayed in *Krasnaia niva* and *Atelier*. At the Paris Exhibition of 1925 she exhibited her own embroidery in a geometric style for table linens as well as designs for printing and embroidery. They were distinguished by a firm constructive and compositional foundation and an intuitive, decorative touch.

124

Her acquaintance with costume began with her theater designs prior to the revolution. At the Moscow Chamber Theater, beginning in 1915, she executed costumes for Sem Benelli's unrealized drama *The Supper of Jokes*, for the play *The Rose and the Cross* based on Alexandr Blok's poems, the stage design and costumes for the play on the theme of the Indian epic *Nala and Damayanti*, and many others. Her work for the theater developed her plastic gift, her ability to "sculpt" the costume. Her sketches reveal unusual confidence and precision, and an ability not merely to design the outfit but to somehow suggest the personality of its future wearer.

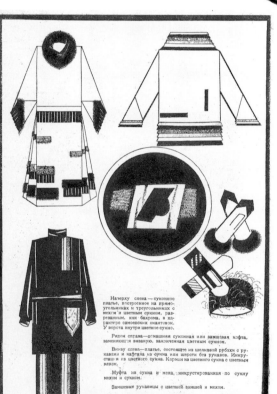

126

125

Anonymous artist. Sketches of
costumes, mittens, and muffs
printed in the magazine *Krasnaia
niva*. 1923.

126

P. Snopkov. sketches of
spetsodezhda (work clothes)
printed in *Krasnaia niva*. 1923.

127

S. Chekhonin. Sketch of a fan.
1923. The fan ushered in a new
epoch in the history of Soviet
costume, when after long
discussions on hygienic and
comfortable clothes for work,
elegant garments came back in
vogue. NEP temporarily revived
trade, the production of goods,
and a high standard of living.

128

O. Anisimova. Sketches of
summer dresses printed in *Atelier*.
1923. All four models were to be
made of homespun fabrics: linen,
loose-weave cloth, and muslin,
and the polka dots were to be
applied with indelible dye.

129

Anonymous artist. Sketches of
costumes in *Atelier*, 1923. The
recommended textiles — knitted
fabrics, crêpe de chine, cheviot
and cashmere — and the fluted
and accordion-pleated skirts all
reveal the source of the
borrowings: European fashion
magazines.

127

The success of the Soviet costume section at the Paris Exposition in 1925, and also the difficulties, which became obvious by the mid-1920s, of carrying out many of the new mass industrial garment projects, induced a number of designers to switch over to handicrafts. Another incentive was an offer by some foreign garment-making firms to exhibit Russian costume designs based on folk motifs in America and in Italy. We know about this from the correspondence between representatives of American firms and Soviet handicraft workshops: Americans offered an exhibition of mass-produced garments, and the Soviets were invited to exhibit articles made with handicraft fabrics along the lines of folk art, as well as samples of industrial products.[43]

In December 1925, a costume section was created specially for this purpose under the Society for the Promotion of Industrial Art Culture. The preparation of the exhibition was entrusted to Lamanova (on behalf of Moscow Garment and Moscow Handicrafts Export), to Mikhailov (on behalf of the State Trade Organization), and to Davydova (on behalf of Moscow Handicrafts Export),[44] with industrial designers invited as well.

Information about this costume section is scarce; apparently it did not last long, and unfortunately, the exchange exhibits between America and Russia did not take place.[45]

In the second half of the 1920s, Evgeniia Pribylskaia rose to prominence among garment designers. She was not as important a designer as Lamanova, but was rightfully considered the top expert in handmade embroidery and homespun textiles. She was closely connected with the Handicrafts Export and the Museum of Handicrafts, and was active in the work of the handicrafts section of the State Academy of Artistic Sciences and, later, of the Institute of Art Industry. Despite her specialization, Pribylskaia was not unconcerned with the basic problems of clothes design, and created samples of clothes in which she used folksy trimmings and embroideries. She was aware that "at the present time embroidery cannot be an end in itself, its position is determined by the epoch, which does not permit . . . production of labor-intensive and expensive articles of a useless nature."[46]

With the development of new forms of functional costume, the nature

43.
GAKhN, f. 941, op. 3, d. 57.

44.
GAKhN, f. 941, op. 3, d. 58.

45.
From GAKhN data (f. 941, op. 15, d. 29) we know that the USSR took part in the International Exhibition in Italy in 1924.

46.
E. Pribylskaia, "Vyshivka v nastoiashchem proizvodstve" in Atelier, 1923, no. 1, p. 7.

130

131

130, 131
Summer dresses and light
overcoats for spring and autumn
wear of the early 1920s.

132
Comfortable pajamas to lounge in
the countryside after work. Early
1920s.

133, 134
Woman's beach costume and
fashionable men's and women's
garments of the early 1920s.

of ornamentation was bound to change as well. For an artist who wholly adopted Nadezhda Lamanova's principles of clothing design, the new types of ornamentation applied to both mass-produced clothes and made-to-order dresses. Since the opportunities for industrial production of clothes in the mid-1920s were so limited, Pribylskaia was compelled to make ornaments mostly at a small workshop, using homespun fabrics. Yet on the whole she retained her approach to dress design as an industrial artist. She often confirmed this in her articles in the journals, and in her report "Homespun Textiles and Embroidery in Contemporary Women's Clothes" at the meeting of the handicrafts section of the State Academy of Artistic Sciences in 1928.[47] This report is a unique and important document in the history of Soviet costume for its original approach to the problem of integrating hand embroidery into the shape and construction of the new costume: "Handmade embroidery and lace are important today. The manufacturing industry has developed standards involving the possibilities of machinery, and these standards have influenced the place of handiwork in tailoring homespun fabrics.

"After the war the types of handmade embroidery for dresses changed, owing to the new forms of the clothing. This was the beginning of an organic connection between shape and fabric in contemporary clothes. The attention given to the constructive element in women's dress has spawned the new view of both the embroidery and the dress not as trimming or ornamentation but, to a certain extent, as a constructive and finishing material.

"The European costume is hampered by embellishing elements that do not serve its construction, but its appearance. They are not clear enough in construction.

"The construction of a costume is based on a correct division of the human figure and a clear conception of its main scheme of movement. Geometrization of the forms makes it possible to conceive the plan that the work will follow.

"The core of the work in the laboratories is not the development of a standard but the development of firm principles on which clothes and their decoration rest."[48]

47.
TsGALI, f. 941, op. 48, d. 7 (protokol 5. Doklad na kustarnoi sektsii ot 21. XII. 1928).

48.
Ibid.

Pribylskaia's report complemented and explained a number of principles of Lamanova's program. Both artists believed that the ornamentation depended on the form of the garment and that the nature of the fabric clued the embroiderer both to the type of the pattern and its design. In Pribylskaia's words, "the embroidery constructs the dress together with the material." The new chemise silhouette was one of the most geometrized forms, in which the "bulk" of the ornament and its character could be precisely defined. The embroidery helped to conceal the defects of the factory-made fabric of the time — dull and poorly dyed — and sounded the garment's main decorative note. Pribylskaia explained: "Owing to the absence of new kinds of textiles and to the extremely scant choice of fabrics, embroidery can be employed partly to finish the fabric. It can have a utilitarian significance, raising the textural value of the fabric by turning it into a more elegant material. It can thus help us to achieve the desired goals for future improvements in textiles."[49]

The artist believed in functional costume in which the rules of correlation between shape, fabric, and ornament were logically observed. Therefore, when choosing her embroidery motifs, Pribylskaia sought simple forms, whether variations of fold designs, simplified Art Nouveau patterns, or a constructivist style with geometricized forms.

Pribylskaia and Lamanova created an exhibit for the 1928 exhibition of Homespun Fabrics and Hand-Made Embroidery in Modern Costume. Their cooperation can be regarded as one of the first major joint efforts between Soviet textile and costume designers. Of great interest among Pribylskaia's works is the dress with motifs of the "Uzbek abroma": this model was one of the first in Soviet fashion in which use was made of

49.
E. Pribylskaia, "Vyshivka v nastoiashchem proizvodstve." *Atelier*, 1923, no. I, p. 7.

132

Central Asian textile designs. The dress is a straight, loose chemise with wide sleeves and a low neck. Three ornamental stripes run along its front, and the outer two, crossing at the shoulder, continue along the back. When making models for international exhibitions, Pribylskaia often complicated ornamental motifs so that they covered a larger surface than usual, and thus looked even more intricate and attractive.

Alexandra Exter's career as an artist did not immediately suggest an inclination for clothing design. A professional painter, Exter showed an early gift as a colorist. Her work in the then-fashionable style of cubism displays special attention to color, which became the artist's vehicle for vivid and dynamic decoration. Her canvases are saturated with extraordinary combinations of violet, cherry, orange, and deep blue. Yakov Tugendkhold, who researched her works, wrote: "Her cubistic canvases are conceived as carpets, every thread rich with color."[50]

50.
Ya. Tugendkhold. *Alexandra Exter kak zhivopisets i khudozhnik stseny*. Berlin, Zarya, 1922, p. 7.

133

Exter also worked for the theater: in 1915 she began to design the decor and costumes for plays produced at the Moscow Chamber Theater.[51] Some of her experiments involved three-dimensional scenery design. She even painted the walls of the theater's foyer and made the curtain, in an attempt to create a unified artistic environment.

51.
These included the plays *Famira Kilfarel* by I. Annensky, *Romeo and Juliet* by William Shakespeare, and *Salome* by Oscar Wilde.

At the beginning of the 1920s, Exter, like Mukhina and many other artists, was filled with a desire to involve herself in all fields of creative activity: "She was drawn toward the stage by the spirit of the times — it was new and required a wider range than easel painting."[52] She plunged into the vast sphere of "making things," and in 1923 began designing everyday costume in earnest. Her wide-

52.
Ya. Tugendkhold. *Alexandra Exter kak zhivopisets i khudozhnik stseny*, p.7.

ranging talent attracted the attention of architects as well: in 1923 she and Ignatii Nivinsky were employed to supervise the decorative color scheme in the pavilions of the All-Russian Agricultural Exhibition in Moscow.

Tugendkhold and other researchers of Exter's art stressed the importance she attached to the "three-dimensional" costume: she tried to exaggerate the three dimensions of the human figure so that it could be lifelike and impressive from all angles. The "three-dimensional" figure, as she saw it, included the "outlines of the figure, its volume and the folds of the dress," which in sketches looked like a rigid frame.

Her stage costumes are larger than life, dynamic characterizations. The peculiarities of these costumes must be analyzed in conjunction with the story of the play and its characters. Definite personalities emerged from the sketches executed in a painterly cubist style. This style was developed by the artist in easel painting and applied to stage costume design. These sketches are far more than working drawings, and should rather be regarded as finished pieces with their own integrity and extraordinary color combinations. Exter's view of the stage costume sketch as a specific and largely independent art was as innovative as all her other theater activities. This is what Tugendkhold said about Exter's stage designs: "She sees costumes as make-up for the body, as a mask for the figure; each of her costumes is conceived as coherent and complete from head (or even from the feather in the cap) to toe. . . ."[53]

134

The artist's approach to the creation of stage costume corresponds to her concept of everyday dress design. Her work had two sides: practical, everyday designs, and elegant couture. The two, however, do not give the impression of

53.
Ya. Tugendkhold.
Alexandra Exter kak zhivopisets i khudozhnik stseny, p. 25.

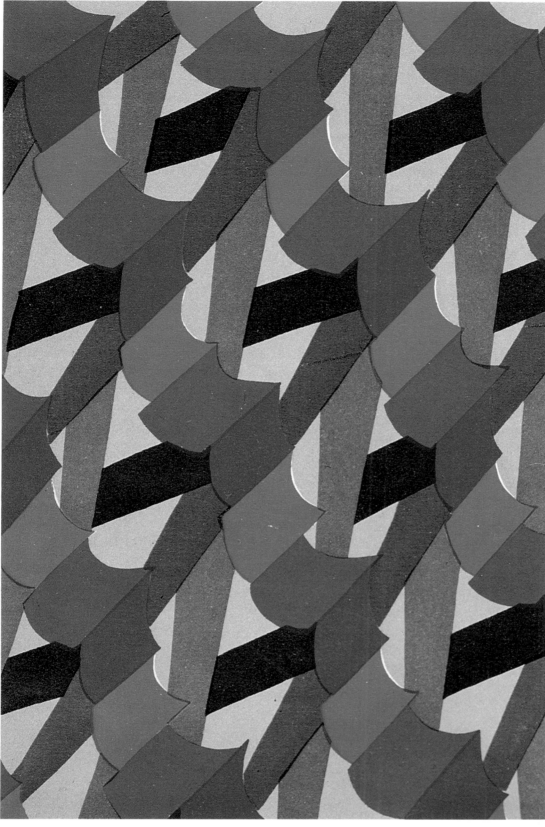

135

Aleksandra Exter (1882-1949)

Aleksandra Aleksandrovna Exter, maiden name Grigorovich, was born in the city of Byelostok near Kiev. She attended art school in Kiev until 1907, and in 1908-1914 continued her studies at the Henri Caraux-Delvai studio of the Grande Chaumiere Academy in Paris. It was during this time that she made the acquaintance of Pablo Picasso, Georges Braque, G. Apollinaire and M. Jacob. In 1909-1915 she lived successively in Paris, Kiev, and Moscow, and travelled to Italy.

In 1919 she took part in the cubist artists' exhibitions in Moscow.

In 1921 Exter worked with a group of constructivist artists designing *prozodezhda* and a new contemporary fashionable costume at the Atelier of Fashions, and wrote articles on the subject.

In 1916-1922 she made innovative sketches of costumes and stage sets for the plays produced by the Moscow Chamber Theater and the Moscow Art Theater (*Famira Kifared* by I. Annensky, Shakespeare's *Romeo and Juliet*, *Salome* by Oscar Wilde, and others).

In 1918-1920 she taught at her own studio in Kiev, and in 1921-1922, at the Higher State Technical Art Studios in Moscow.

In 1923 Exter travelled to France and Italy. She participated in the designing of several pavilions of the Exhibition of Achievements of the National Economy with I. Nivinsky in 1923. She also worked in industrial design.

From 1925 on she lived in Paris, sketched costumes for ballets in Paris, London and Cologne, and taught at the Fernand Leger Academy of Modern Art.

135
A. Exter. Textile design. 1923.

136
Alexandra Exter, painter, graphic artist, stage and textile designer. 1910s.

137
A. Exter. Sketch of a costume for the play *Famira Kifared* by I. Annensky, at the Moscow Chamber Theater. 1916.

being poles apart. As is clear from the views Exter expressed in her articles, she was a confirmed follower of Lamanova's principles. Convinced of the beauty of simple work clothes, she offered models of *prozodezhda*, sports and business clothes, as well as children's garments, based on the principles of comfort, practicality, and versatility.

She articulated her views on new costume design in the article "Simplicity and Practicality in Clothes." "The pace of contemporary life requires the least expenditure of time and effort on production. To contemporary "fashion," which changes at the whim of the businessman [i.e., NEP fashion], we must respond with clothes that are expedient and beautiful in their simplicity. Dress for mass production and wear must consist of simple geometric forms such as the rectangle, square, and triangle; the rhythm of color imparted to them diversifies the form. Made of the plainest materials (canvas, sateen, loose-weave cloth, homespun silk, raw silk, and woollen cloth), these clothes, easily modified, are not monotonous, and the wearer can at any time, if he wishes,

136

54.
A. Exter, "Prostota i praktichnost v odezhde" in *Krasnaia niva*, 1923, no. 21, p. 31.

change both the silhouette of the clothes and their color, because the color of their components is different."[54]

Her garments displayed somewhat unorthodox geometric design and ornament. Their silhouettes formed a rectangle (which followed the general fashion trend); the sleeve was a square or rectangle; the neckline was square or V-shaped; the decorative details were most often small colored rounds or rhombs appliquéd to the fabric. This peculiarity of the artist's garments was pointed out by Tugendkhold: "Exter's costumes are not drawn, but constructed from various surfaces."[55] This is probably the influence of cubist painting — again, elements of the artist's canvases seem to have been transferred to her clothing designs.

55.
Ya. Tugendkhold, *Alexandra Exter kak zhivopisets i khudozhnik stseny*, p. 25.

Of paramount importance in Exter's industrial clothes design was the practicality of the costume. Geometric forms were the easiest for industrial production, and could be mass produced despite the primitive garment technology of the 1920s. Exter's works include the simple and austere office dress, sports coat and jacket, and children's frocks. An especially rational construction is exhibited in the sketch of a man's short coat that widened slightly toward the hem, made of canvas or unbleached linen, i.e., of the cheapest and most accessible materials. The coat's perfect proportions are emphasized by the effective use of texture (on the collar, pockets and sleeves the pattern has one diagonal, and on the remaining parts, another). The beauty of this model lies in the logic of its cut: the size of the square patch pockets, the proportions of the upper section and the height of the stand-up collar. This model ranks with the best examples of 1920s costume art. It is not surprising that this type of sports jacket did not go out of style in subsequent decades and exists to this day. And details (both utilitarian and decorative) like the double row of wooden buttons in the form of vertical sticks are still used in sports clothes.

The artist displayed greater freedom in models of women's dress design, and made the geometrized proportions and forms more complex, introducing yokes and devising new methods of sewing in sleeves and decorative details.

An important area of the costume designer's activities, Exter believed,

137

56.
A. Exter, "V konstruktivnoi odezhde" in *Atelier*, 1923, no. 1, pp. 4-5.

57.
Ibid.

was *prozodezhda*, or work clothes. The principles of their treatment were "expediency, hygiene, nature, psychology and harmony of proportions of the human body."[56] This idea was expressed during the same years by the constructivist artists Popova and Stepanova, and earlier by Lamanova. Defining the role of *prozodezhda*, the artist wrote: "A new uniform is the order of the day. . . . Since the working people form the overwhelming majority in our country, clothes must be adapted to their needs and to the type of work they are doing."[57]

Exter believed that working conditions should dictate the specificity of work clothes; quite naturally, the miner's *prozodezhda* cannot be the same as that worn by the steel founder, and the physician's gown cannot resemble the work clothes of the shop assistant or builder. These ideas were to become a reality much later, when living conditions improved and the level of production rose.

138, 139
A. Exter. Sketches of a coat and dress. 1923.

140
A. Exter. Sketch of a costume for the play *Romeo and Juliet*. 1921. Exter, the already recognized painter and graphic artist, became famous through her work in 1916-1922 at the Moscow Chamber Theater of Alexandr Tairov. One of its most sensational hits was the performance of Shakespeare's *Romeo and Juliet*, for which Exter made three-dimensional scenery and costumes of dazzling beauty. The sketch of Romeo's costume is distinguished by dynamic painterly surfaces and a complexity of green hues. Her theatrical work also left its imprint on the art of everyday costume. Sketches of a costume and a coat of 1923 are characterized by paradoxical correlations of volumes, rhythms and color.

138
139

Рис. 1. А. Экстер. 1923 г.

140

Exter often worked side by side with Lamanova and Mukhina, and their ideas largely coincided. Lamanova's theory of interconnection between the material and form was examined by Exter in much detail. In her article "Constructive Clothes" she analyzed the properties of fabric as diverse as coarse and fine wool and silk, each of which dictates a specific shape. Coarse woollen cloth requires "a form enclosed in a rectangle or constructed on right angles without the unnecessary vertical rhythm of pleats. Soft fabrics (such as wool or silk when properly processed) allow a more complex and diversified silhouette. . . . Elastic fabrics . . . offer an opportunity to make clothes that move (for dancing) and for more complicated forms (a circle or polyhedron)."[58] But, as was mentioned above, in her designs for made-to-order dresses Exter showed a different side of her art. Her works for the Atelier of Fashions can hardly be called everyday clothes — they are more like theater costumes. Although she mostly retained the "modish" silhouette and construction elements (the shape of the sleeves, the neckline) of the period, Exter departed from the laws of construction of everyday dress: the strict proportions, logical cut, and consideration of the material's properties. Disregarding the latter, the artist cut the surface into arbitrarily chosen planes: diamond-shaped, rectangular, or triangular, each differing in texture, pattern, and color. Diagonal lines crossed the dress haphazardly, creating a plethora of geometric shapes.

In these experiments the artist was trying for a stunning effect, through a decorative composition of paradoxical correlations and interconnections of volumes, linear rhythms and colors; i.e., through the formal aspects of her easel painting. These designs possessed an expressive imagery, striking individuality of

58.
A. Exter, "V konstruktivnoi odezhde" in *Atelier*, 1923, no. 1, pp. 4-5.

141

141

A. Exter. Sketch of a costume for
Romeo and Juliet. 1921.

142

A. Exter. Sketch of the costume
for Salome in the play *Salome*
by Oscar Wilde at the Moscow
Chamber Theater. 1921. Somewhat
harsh, the costume, constructed of
fan-shaped forms, attracts by its
beautiful color.

style and their own inner logic. In these clothes the artist proceeded from the same principle as her theater costumes: predominant in them were original stylizations of the then-fashionable Egyptian motifs; sometimes they displayed the saturated color rhythms of Renaissance art. But none of these costumes was a mere copy of the historical — they were conceived and expressed in the language of an artist of the 1920s. Exter was the first in the Soviet art of dress design to draw on the historical costume of different epochs and countries as a source of inspiration for her contemporary clothes. Here she differed from Lamanova, who was attracted more by Russian folk costume. There is only one feature in common between this type of Exter's costume and everyday clothes — their multilayered effect.

Her patterns for tailor-made dresses, ordered by the Atelier of Fashions, were supplied with detailed instructions on which fabrics, furs, trimmings and colors should be used. Here is an example: "A two-piece Sunday dress. The under section with wide sleeves is made of pale violet silk cloth. The cuffs are trimmed with sand-colored leather. The other piece of the dress (a sort of sleeveless jacket) is made of suede or cloth of golden color; a broad double-sided belt of gold and violet tones and the hem are ornamented with leather insets. The collar is a scarf."

Exter chose for such patterns only expensive fabrics, leather, and animal pelts. She combined materials varied in texture and visual effect: silk, satin, brocade, and fur. The eccentricity of her works is revealed, above all, through refined color combinations — plum, orange, black, crimson, violet, ash-grey. Exter showed some of these works at the First All-Russian Industrial Art Exhibition of 1923 organized by the State Academy of Artistic Sciences, and several of Exter's models received prizes. Why complicated, labor-intensive, made-to-order garments obviously intended for the rich would be awarded prizes in this period of Soviet history is indeed a mystery, but perhaps the jury was affected by the aesthetic merits of the dresses, by their qualities as works of art. Although Exter's designs were far removed from the objectives of mass production, they represent the prototype of the so-called "show fashion," which three and a half decades later was to secure for itself a legitimate place in Soviet clothes design.

143

143-145

A. Exter. Sketches of elegant
dresses and an everyday costume.
1923. The sphere of "making
things" attracted Alexandra Exter
because of her "instinct for
contemporaneity, and because
she needed a wider scope than
painting or stage design." Exter
joined the group of constructivists
and wrote articles that had the
ring of manifestos: "Simplicity and
Practicality in Clothes,"
"Constructive Clothes." How
functional, however, is an
asymmetrical dress with a train
and drapery, trimmed with fur?

144

145

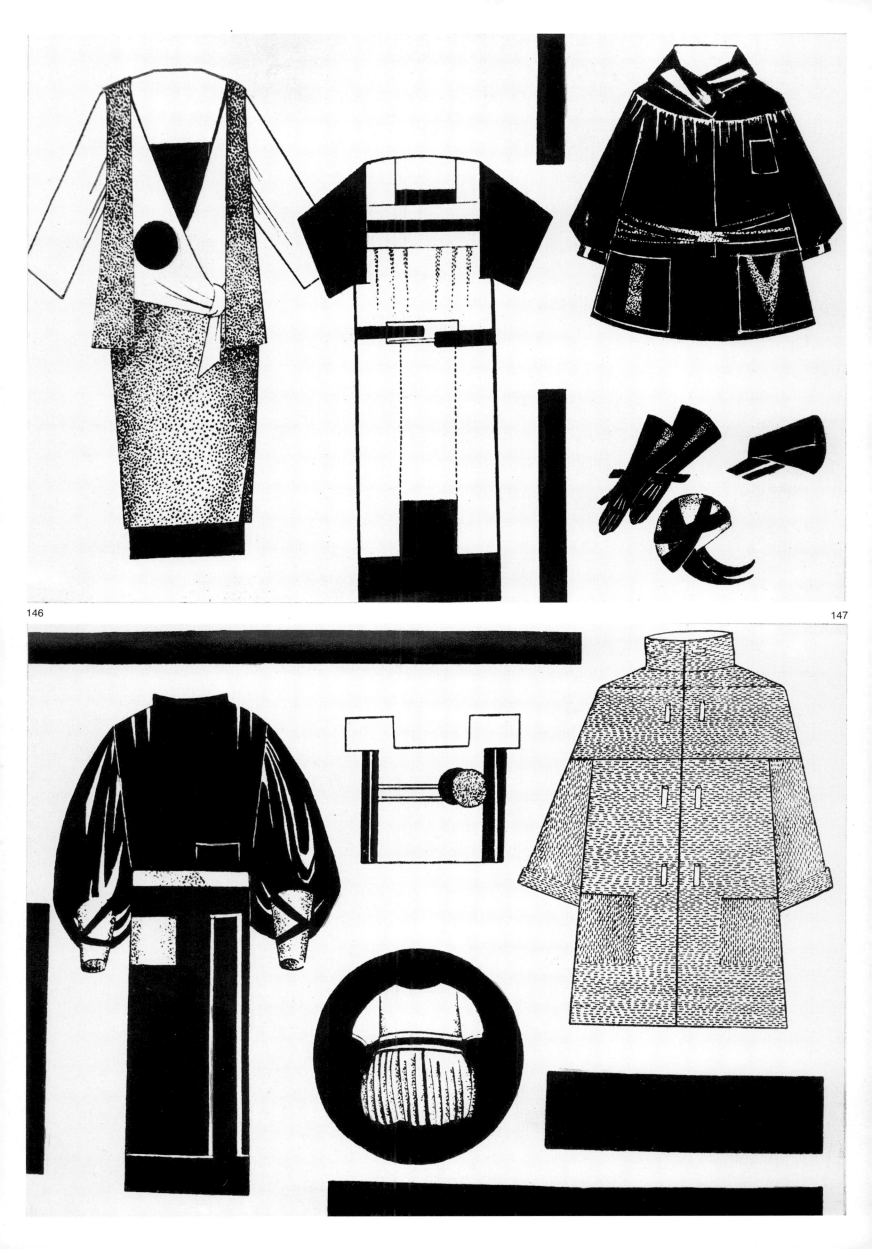

We can judge Alexandra Exter's creative legacy by her sketches of dresses intended for daily wear published in 1920s periodicals. Here as well she attached importance to the humanistic and emotional aspect of the sketch, in her depiction of the model's pose, gestures, "arrested" movement, and the harmony between the costume and the figure. In this sense one can speak of a gallery of characters of Exter's sketches, which clearly reveal a kinship with the theatrical heroes of her works. It was only in the 1960s that such an attitude to clothes design became widespread; it was initiated, no doubt, by Exter.

While certain difficulties were inevitable in executing theater costumes after the artist's sketches, it was different with the realization of the costumes for Protazanov's film *Aelita*. Here, all the peculiarities of the author's designs were retained. The producer understood Exter's desire to construct a complicated, somewhat irrational costume, as well as her love of unusual materials. Her inclinations corresponded to those of

146, 147

A. Exter. Sketches of mass-produced clothes. 1923. Practical and functionally expedient, these clothes could be manufactured on a factory conveyer belt. At the same time the artist tried to individualize garments, which is evident from the modern-looking ornamental elements. The sketches were printed in *Atelier*.

148

Dress after A. Exter's sketch in 1923. Reconstruction made in 1979.

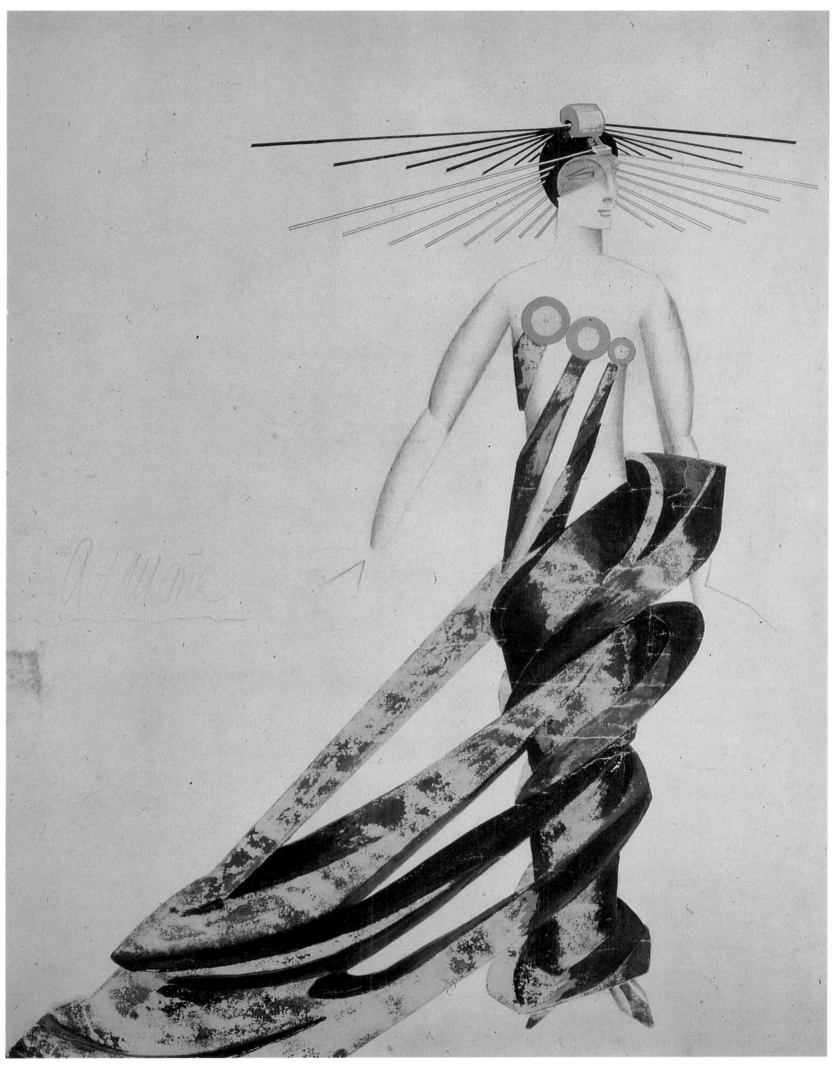

149
A. Exter. Sketch of Aelita's
costume for the film of the same
title by Ya. Protazanov. 1924.

150, 151
Frames from the film *Aelita*. 1924.

Protazanov — to create not ordinary "earthly" costumes (in fact, they were for extra-terrestrials!), but quite unique pieces in which the artist's fancy could take flight. To accomplish such a task textiles alone were not enough, so the author used an unusual rigid frame of transparent plastic and metal. Costumes made from these constructions were voluminous and elastic, their imagery suggesting the mysterious realm of a strange, remote planet.

Still another master of costume, Nadezhda Makarova, started her career at the Workshops of Contemporary Dress under the guidance of Lamanova, whom she had admired since she was a child. In fact she was only a child when she began working there. Makarova's designs clearly were influenced by Lamanova's theories: they were austere, chemise-style dresses made of canvas and linen, decorated with bright, multi-colored stripes and insets based on folk motifs. Not infrequently, Makarova used the very same border of old-fashioned towels and napkin details, but more often she integrated creatively reinterpreted elements of folk ornament. Affinity with Russian folk clothes is found in many of Makarova's works: a white linen dress is cut in the form of a straight chemise, a gusset in red (one of the characteristic features of folk models) is stitched into the sleeve, the high line of the sewn-in sleeve is accented with an ornamental border, and the round neck and the hemline are trimmed in red. The bodice has a small ornamental inset. Makarova

showed herself a devotee of folk costume in the cut, the placing of color accents, and the combining of traditional Russian hues.

By the mid-1920s, the designer was already unveiling the characteristic features of her individual style: the striving for simplicity and elegance in austere and logical forms, and in laconic but bright color combinations. Whereas Lamanova liked to assemble a costume of several pieces — a caftan, skirt, and blouse — using parts of finished folk articles (towels, homespun skirts and napkins), Makarova soon lost interest in these experiments. She introduced decorative patches into the very construction of the model — into the sides up to the armhole or into the jacket fronts or skirt panels. Often these were unornamented insets of vivid color. Graceful proportions distinguish a simple white dress: short, sleeveless, with a round neckline, and with rectangular red inserts on the bodice and from the hips to the hemline.

Makarova occasionally used a multitude of colors in a costume, but usually preferred a two- or three-color range (the principle of Russian folk costume). One of the artist's best works of the mid-1920s was an ensemble consisting of a straight sleeveless dress and a long straight vest, with the armholes, belt, and pockets edged in blue. The ornamented surface, the rhythm of the pattern, and the color distribution reveal a desire to attain harmony with the proportion and construction of the dress as a whole.

At the Exposition internationale des arts décoratifs, held in Paris in 1925, Makarova showed two ensembles that combined the features of the fashionable trend of those years (a straight silhouette, skirts ending at the knee) with the traditional Russian shape and decorative trim. Like many other designs by Russian designers, they included long straight jackets worn over the dresses. The jacket, made of black cashmere, was decorated with a narrow band of floral ornament bordering the breast and the upper part of the back. The white linen caftan in another ensemble can also be categorized as a design based on folk motifs. By the end of the 1920s, the artist showed a definite tendency toward simplifying her cut and using the least possible length of fabric and time on its manufacture, while trying nevertheless to heighten the dress's constructive and decorative expressiveness.

152

152, 153

Frames from the film *Aelita*.
The part of Aelita was played by
Yulia Solntseva, a silent film star.
The film was based on Alexei
Tolstoy's novel (1922), which
enjoyed unprecedented popularity.
The scenery representing the
martians' dwellings was made
by Isaac Rabinovich and Viktor
Simov. Alexandra Exter imagined
clothes of the future for her
costumes.

153

155

Nadezhda Makarova (1898-1969)

Nadezhda Sergeievna Makarova was
born in Moscow. After graduation from
high school she worked as a teacher in
the Kaluga province. On her return to
Moscow she lived with N. Lamanova,
helping her in her dressmaker shop.
In 1923-1924 Makarova attended K.
Yuon's studio of painting, simultaneously
working as an artist at the Workshops of
Contemporary Dress, and from 1927 she
worked at the Kustexport Corporation.
In the mid-1920s she began making
theater costumes for plays produced
at the Moscow Art Theatre and the
Meierkhold and Vakhtangov theaters.
In 1934 she became the first art director
of the Moscow (later All-Union) House of
Clothing Design (1934-1938 and
1945-1949). Makarova actively
participated in the creation in Moscow of
the All-Union Institute of Assortment of
Light Industry.
N. Makarova consistently followed
N. Lamanova's principles of designing
functional, simple and comfortable
clothing for mass production.

Makarova enthusiastically worked at that time on dress and coat designs in view of mass production. One of these was the well-known and popular straight coat made of checked material, which was produced at one of the Moscow factories at the end of the 1920s. Thanks to its harmonious proportions and its classically Russian cut derived from folk design, this coat was later repeatedly produced in series, and even now does not look old-fashioned. It appears to be one of the first and few examples of a high aesthetic quality produced by the industry in those years.

Makarova's interpretation of the concept of "simplicity" in a dress was this: "I believe that real simplicity (which is not vulgarization, of course) and a natural, non-artificial form express the true elegance of costume, are alien to mannerism, and are always a sign of good taste. I see these qualities in the best works of decorative art and of folklore."[59]

A thorough exploration of the principles of logic in the cut led Makarova, like Lamanova, to the idea of variability. Without changing the con-

59.
Notes of N. Makarova. Manuscript. Archives of T. Strizhenova.

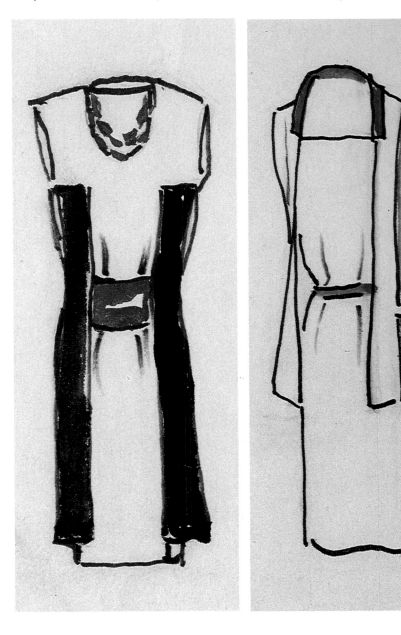

154
N. Makarova. Sketch of a summer ensemble. Late 1920s.

155
Nadezhda Makarova in the 1920s.

156, 157
N. Makarova. Sketches of costume of the 1920s. Lamanova's niece did not learn the art of clothes design from textbooks. At first she did the hemming and overstitching in Lamanova's workshop, then modelled her costumes. Her own early designs reflected her teacher's tastes, as evident in the white dress with the black insets at the sides.

156
157

159

1925

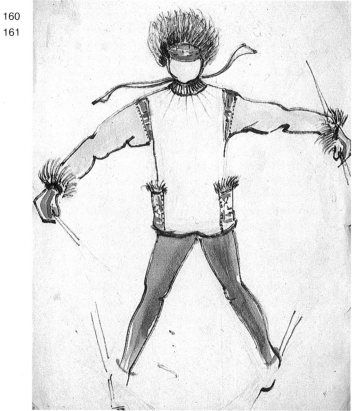

160
161

158

N. Makarova. Sketch of a children's winter costume. Early 1930s.

159

N. Makarova. Sketch of a woman's short winter coat. 1925.

160

N. Makarova. Sketch of a woman's ski suit. Early 1930s.

161

N. Makarova. Sketch of a woman's coat. 1939. When designing winter clothes, Makarova turned to traditions of the peoples of the North. This is noticeable both in the cut of the 1925 coat and in its decoration: the sleeves, hood, and pockets are trimmed with fur and ornamented with embroidery.

158

162
N. Makarova. Sketch of an autumn costume and a headdress. 1930s.

163
N. Makarova. Sketch of a chemise-style dress with inserts at the sides and a richly ornamented lower section. 1925-1926.

164
N. Makarova. Sketch of a dress. 1920s.

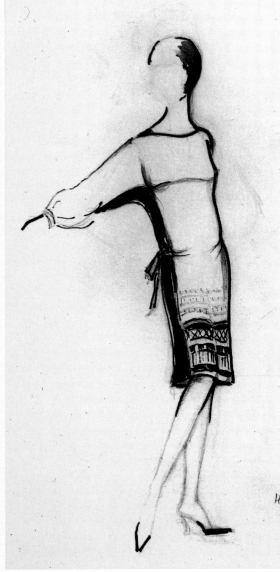

163

struction, the artist created many versions of the garment, transforming its appearance with details: the shape of the collar, the length of the sleeves, and the trim. This method could not be widely applied in mass production in the 1920s, but the very idea of variability was revolutionary, and it has been widely used since the 1960s in Soviet clothes design.

Color, Makarova believed, was tremendously important in clothing. It serves as "the emotional dominant to which all the accessories are subordinated and on which the imagery depends."[60] The artist achieved great emotional expressiveness in her works thanks to her excellent sense of color. She was also fond of combinations of black and white and shades of gray, discovering in a monochrome range a singular refinement and elegance. Her percipience was confirmed; as the history of fashion shows, combinations of these shades recur more often than any others.

Not infrequently the artist drew inspiration from nature: flowers, birds, butterflies, animals; their shapes and colors were skillfully and imaginatively applied to garments. A flower's petals prompted a pattern of skirts for little girls, and the shapes of small animal heads were used in children's headwear. Nevertheless, throughout the 1920s, especially when working on handcrafted dresses with Lamanova, Makarova's most extensively used motif was that of Russian folk costume.

This group of talented artists influenced by the leader of modern Soviet costume design, Nadezhda Lamanova, though differing from each other in style and approach, firmly agreed on the main purpose of Soviet clothes design: to create functional forms of costume based on new aesthetic principles, for the new mass consumer, the worker.

60.
Notes of N. Makarova.

165

166

Constructivist Design

The artists grouped around the magazine *Lef* [Left Front of Arts], such as Liubov Popova, Varvara Stepanova, Alexandr Rodchenko, the Vesnin brothers, Alexandr and Viktor, and others who designed new types of contemporary clothes in the early 1920s, were a unique phenomenon. All started their careers in art as painters, graphic artists, or architects. Many of them, however, came to believe that in a revolutionary epoch easel painting had less meaning than socially useful work in industry. They turned to the creation of a new costume, for they were sure that it was a domain in which they could apply their talent and knowledge as truly revolutionary artists.

The constructivist artists attempted to apply the ideas and methods of their art to the design of mass-produced consumer goods. Their motives were described by Karl Kantor: "After the arrogant, scornful attitude toward work that was cultivated by official, aristocratic and bourgeois society, after its contempt of material and industrial activity as unaesthetic, after the idealistic eulogizing of art as a purely spiritual process and the

165

L. Popova. Textile design. 1923.

166

V. Tatlin. Model of a monument to the Third International. 1920. The author of the project, with pipe in hand, stands beside his work.

167

V. Stepanova. Composition of two figures against a circle. 1922. The art of constructivists, who in the early 1920s developed new forms, was an exceptional phenomenon. Alexandr Rodchenko, Vladimir Tatlin, Varvara Stepanova, Liubov Popova, Alexandr Vesnin, and Gustav Klutsis formulated the concept of an artist-constructivist, and made textile and clothes designs, worked for the theater, produced posters and created monuments. Tatlin's monument to the Third International became a symbol of that turbulent epoch.

167

168

170

169

unrestrained policy of individualism in the bourgeois aesthetics of pre-revolutionary years, the 'productionists' have boldly set the task: to promote the world-wide historical process of reuniting art with materially productive work."[61]

In 1923, the newspaper *Pravda* called upon the artists to renovate industrial production. The director of the First Cotton-Printing Factory in Moscow, A. Arkhangelsky, and Professor P. Viktorov, an expert in textile production technology, wrote an article about the boring routine in the factory and the need for radical and urgent change.[62]

61.
K. Kantor, "Sotsialnye osnovy promyshlennogo iskusstva," in the book *Iskusstvo i promyshlennost.* Moscow, 1967, p. 13.

62.
Pravda, June 1923.

171

172

168-172

L. Popova. Textile designs. 1923. Painter Liubov Popova and Varvara Stepanova crossed the threshold of the First Textile Print Factory in 1923. Ornamental patterns for fabrics created by her became works of true industrial art. The constructivist artists offered unusual geometrical ornaments instead of the traditional plant motifs. They did not immediately meet with understanding — their colleagues at the factory rebuked them for drawing "with the help of compasses and a ruler," and claimed they "cannot draw."

Stepanova and Popova immediately responded to the appeal and took employment at the First Cotton-Printing Factory. The artists' first action was a memo to the administration, in which they stressed the importance of creative efforts in the new project and enumerated the conditions required for its radical transformation. Below is the text of the memo:

1. Artists' participation in industrial production, either working closely with or directing the artistic side of things, with the right to vote (on production plans, models for production, acquisition of designs, and hiring of workers in the art sector).
2. Participation in the chemistry laboratory to observe the coloration process.
3. Production of designs for block-printed fabrics.
4. Contact with the sewing workshops, fashion ateliers, and magazines.
5. Access to information at the factories and in the press and advertisements in magazines.[63]

173

63.
A. Lavrentiev, "Poeziia graficheskogo dizaina v tvorchestve Varvary Stepanovoi" in *Tekhnicheskaia estetika*, 1980, no. 5, p. 25.

This novel program embraced, in fact, all aspects of work at the factory. The two artists immediately made an effort to understand the specific technological demands of the industry.

Their actions, as well as those of the factory managers, were dictated by the critical situation in industrial production—nothing had changed in the country's textile mills since the October Revolution. The economic crisis had reduced textile output almost to zero. There was utter stagnation and lack of creativity in the work of the factory designers. The custom of copying foreign patterns (mostly French) had continued for quite a while, but by the time Stepanova and Popova

Liubov Popova (1889-1924)

Liubov Sergeievna Popova was born in the village of Ivanovskoie near Moscow. In 1907-1908 she studied at S. Zhukovsky's painting and drawing studio and at the school of painting and drawing of K. Yuon and I. Dudin. In 1912-1913 she studied at La Palette Academy in Paris and at A. Metzinger's and H. Le Fauconnier's studio. In 1913-1915 she worked at V. Tatlin's studio, Bashnia (The Tower); from 1914 she took part in exhibitions of easel painters, the Knave of Diamonds, Tram V, 5x5=25, and others. In 1914 she travelled to Italy and France.

In 1918 Popova was a member of the board of the Fine Arts Department of the People's Commissariat of Public Education and Professor of the Free Art Studios. From 1920, she was one of the organizers and a member of the Institute of Artistic Culture. In 1921 she was Professor of the Higher State Technical-Art Studios and a member of the editorial board of *Lef* (Left Front of the Arts) magazine. From 1921-1924, she worked at the art studio of the First Textile Print Factory with V. Stepanova. She designed new geometric ornaments for cotton fabrics and women's everyday garments. She also worked as a book designer and made stage and costume designs at the Meierkhold theater. In 1911 she studied Old Russian art in Pskov and Vologda.

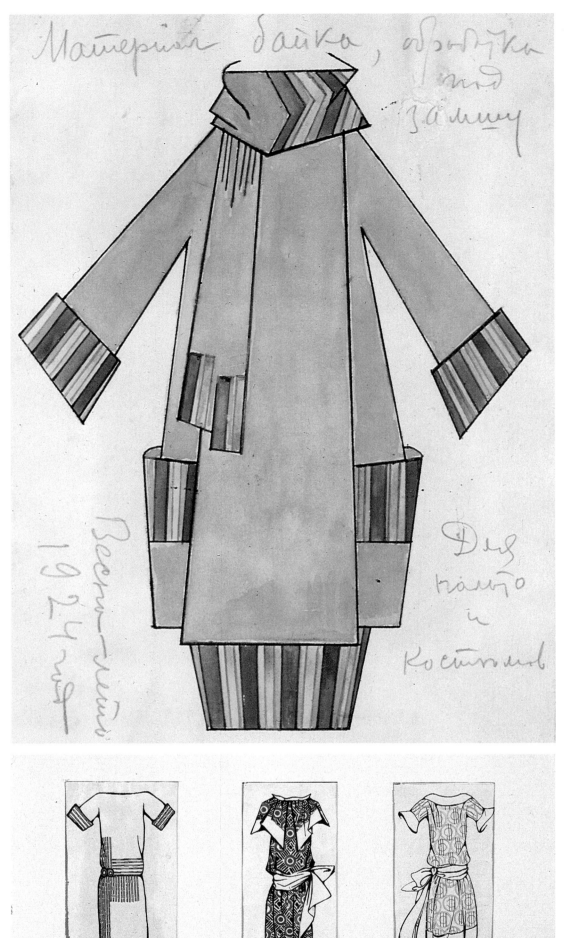

175
176
177
178

173
L. Popova. Sketch of a dress. 1923.

174
Varvara Stepanova and Liubov Popova, friends and co-workers in art, the first "artist-productionists" to work at a factory. 1923. Photo by A. Rodchenko.

175
L. Popova. Sketch of a coat and a costume of thick flannelette. 1924.

176-178
L. Popova. Sketches of dresses. 1923.

arrived, contacts with former suppliers in France had finally been severed. Therefore the factories resumed printing designs from the old plates, with plant motifs predominating. Moreover, the number of textile specialists at the beginning of the 1920s had sharply declined. The lamentable state of cotton printing was described by B. Arvatov at the meeting of the Institute of Artistic Culture in March 1923 after the inspection of the Ivanovo-Voznesensk factories. He said that "the 'aesthetic' side of the trade is entirely out of touch with production. The graphic artists of the old academic, naturalistic school produce designs for calico not only disregarding production but with absolutely no knowledge of it. The design and production departments are worlds apart." Arvatov suggested that artists begin working in the industry and help lead it out of its deadlock; he insisted that experimental laboratories be opened at the factories.[64]

64.
TsGAOR, f. 5721, op. 1, d. 1, pp. 20-20a (account of the report).

Popova and Stepanova showed much energy and persistence in consistently defending their innovative program, and often met with resistance at the factory.

Having studied the technological foundations of the production process, they proposed textile designs that were stylistically new. In this they were helped by their background in easel painting. Stepanova and Popova were adherents of the new painting before the revolution: in the 1910s Popova was a member of the avant-garde Knave of Diamonds society, and Stepanova, somewhat later, exhibited her works with the members of the 5x5=25 exhibition, who also advocated Leftist art. The two artists applied their art to garment design, creating ornaments based on diverse geometric motifs of a planar nature. Their many combinations of geometric forms, sharply contrasting colors, and complex superimposed criss-crossing lines produced a stunning impression of novelty and rich imagination.

The artists were attracted to their work at the factory because of the challenge of applying traditional painting to industrial production and, what was more important, their desire to be useful to the new society. They claimed they considered the creation of drawings for factory calico printing more important than activities in the realm of "pure" art. The

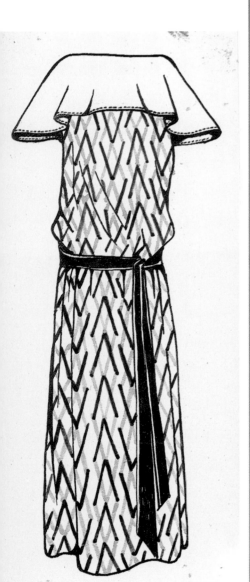

179

180

179
L. Popova. Sketch of a dress.
1923.

180
A dress made after L. Popova's
design of 1923. Reconstruction by
E. Khudiakova (1985), who also
models the dress.

181
A dress made after L. Popova's
design of 1923. Reconstruction
by E. Khudiakova. 1985.

182, 183
L. Popova. Sketches of dresses.
1923.

merging of the artist's creative efforts with modern industry promised an aesthetic transformation of life and work—a dream that the best creative forces of the revolutionary era strived to make a reality. In 1927, Popova and Stepanova's geometric drawing experiments were repeated by the artist Liudmila Maiakovskaia at the Trekhgornaia Textile Mill in Moscow. Although they consisted of only a few samples, the artist's work marked the turning of a page in the early history of Soviet industrial textiles.

In her obituary "In Memory of L. S. Popova" (who died suddenly in 1924) it was written:

"Popova was a constructivist engaged in production not only in words but in deed. When she was invited with Stepanova to work at the former Tsindel factory, she was genuinely thrilled. She pored over designs for calicos, trying to integrate in a single creative act the requirements of economy, the laws of decoration, and the inscrutable taste of the Tula peasant woman. No compliments or flattering offers could tempt her. She categorically declined employment at exhibitions and museums. To 'fathom' the calico was far more attractive to her than to please the aesthetic world of pure art."[65]

65.
"Pamiati L. S. Popovoi" in Lef, 1924, no. 2, p. 3.

Popova and Stepanova created textile designs that had had no analogue in the history of Soviet Russia, and consequently their designs are known as "the first Soviet fashion." Approximately in the same years (1921-1925) experiments with geometric textile ornament were made in France as well by the artists E. Courtod, Paul Poiret, Erté, and Sonia Delaunay. The important difference was, however, that the French experimental samples numbered only a few copies, were intended for the elite, and were developed against the background of the prevailing Art Deco style in clothes.

Popova and Stepanova were convinced that it was precisely this geometric style that was to replace the traditional, and therefore outdated plant motif, or "flowerets."

In her report at the Institute of Artistic Culture, "On the Status and Tasks of a Constructivist Artist in the Cotton Printing Industry, in Connection with the Work at the First Textile Print Factory," Stepanova enumerated the artists' major goals:

66.
TsGAOR, op. 1, d. 1, s. 7,
5 January 1924.

"To eradicate the deep-rooted view of an ideal artistic design as an imitation and reflection of painting. To eliminate the plant motif and replace it with geometrized shapes. To propagate the constructivist's production tasks."[66]

While transferring the fundamentals of geometric painting to fabrics, the artists enhanced their compositional and coloristic clarity and subordinated decoration to the general solution of the design. At that time the designs of Popova and Stepanova were called "nonobjective" — and are still known under this appellation. Constructed as combinations of various geometric lines and figures — circles, zigzags, broken lines, lattices, fly-wheels, and segments of a circle — the ornaments smoothly passed, even flowed, from one form into another, or abruptly and unexpectedly crossed, or ran parallel in rhythmic patterns. They sometimes reveal an obvious influence of machine industry, denoted in the press by the term "machinism." Industrial motifs—cogs, wheels, and levers—often figured in their designs.

New emblems like the hammer and sickle or five-pointed star, rhythmically recurring on the surface of the fabric, were also used. The ground often remained white, with intense designs of saturated black and red, sometimes augmented with blue or green.

Most of the artists' designs were simple and uncomplicated, and were easily mass produced. Their best works exhibit an acute sense of beauty of geometrized forms, rhythms, juxtaposition of contrasting colors, and a conception of planar ornament: they had an unprecedented ability to produce an impression of flatness even when the design was multilayered.

Popova and Stepanova were the first Soviet designers to attempt to design both fabric and clothes. Their lack of experience in clothing design surfaced at the factory, where many of their projects for mass production were rejected, for they would have required major alterations to the conveyor system. An all too clear lack of understanding of the artists' innovative efforts was recorded by Stepanova in her notebook "Registration of Textile Samples." Factory councils "proposed that constructivism should be covered with a veil of fancy, only then will the designs

184-186

L. Popova. Sketches of *prozodezhda* (professional garments) for actors. No. 7, nc. 4, no. 2. 1921. For the constructivists, theater was both the laboratory and the workplace; that is where they experimented with their ideas. The painter Liubov Popova left her canvases and came to the theater "to escape from the deadlock of representation," as she put it. The premiere of *The Magnanimous Cuckold* produced in 1922 by V. S. Meierkhold, with the settings designed by Popova, started the history of theatrical constructivism. A structure representing a mill was erected on the stage and the characters were clothed in costumes which Popova called "the actor's *prozodezhda*." It is remarkable that the costumes were designed not only for this particular play but also for wear in everyday life, during the rehearsals and at home. Her sketches of actors' *prozodezhda* were used by Popova as visual aids for students, who she taught as the lecturer in "Costume as an Element of Theatrical Design" at V. Meierkhold's Free Studios under the State Higher Theatrical Studios in 1921.

184

185
186

187

188

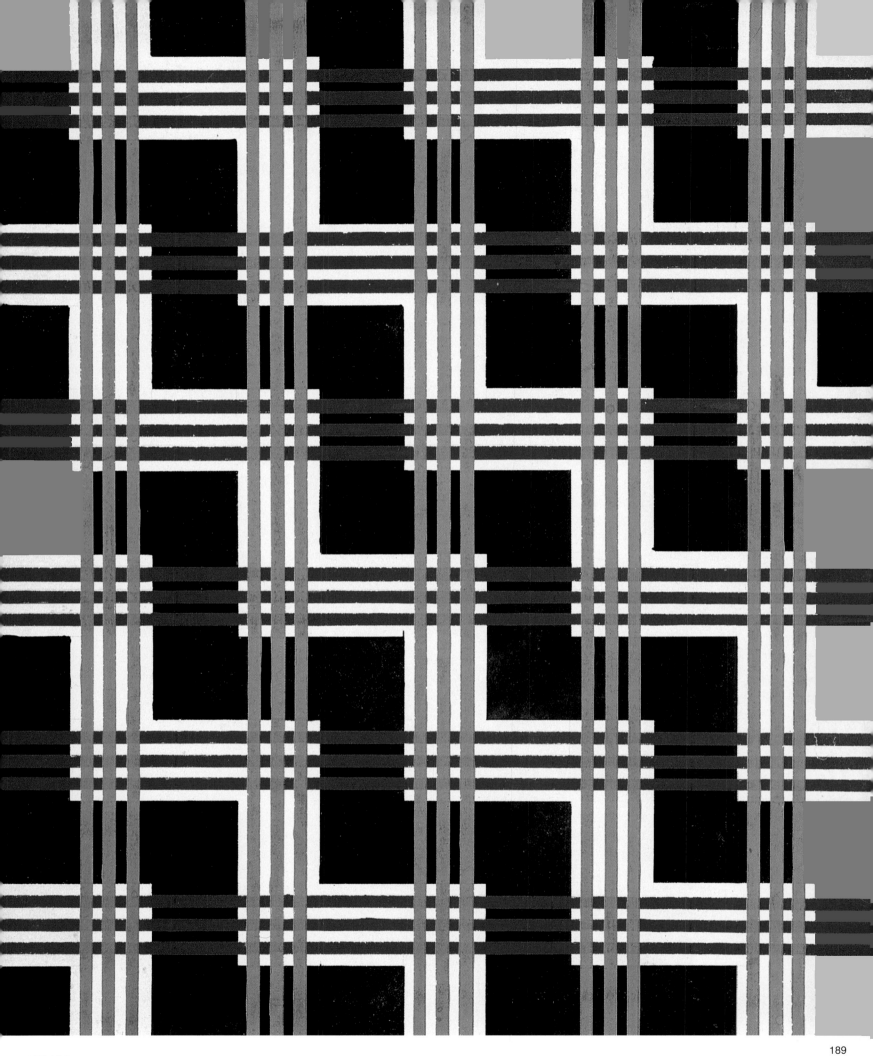

187-189

V. Stepanova. Fabric designs.

1924.

190

190

V. Stepanova. Fabric design. 1924.

191-192

Varvara Stepanova in a uniform cap for State Publishing House salesmen. She wears a dress made of a fabric of her own design. Photo by A. Rodchenko. 1924.

193-195

V. Stepanova. Fabric designs. 1924. At the First Textile Print Factory Stepanova created over a hundred designs for textiles. The artist enjoyed seeing her calicos worn, and claimed that not a single exhibition of her paintings gave her as much pleasure.

191

Varvara Stepanova (1894-1958)

Varvara Fedorovna Stepanova was born in the city of Kovno (Kaunas) in Lithuania. She studied at the art school in Kazan until 1912 and then at the school-studios of I. Mashkov and K. Yuon. In 1913-1914 she attended the Moscow Industrial Art School.

Beginning in 1914 she participated in easel painters' exhibitions, including the "5x5=25" constructivists' exhibition in 1921, and the international exhibition of decorative art in Paris in 1925. She also showed at the First Exhibition of Russian Art in Berlin in 1922.

In 1918 Stepanova became a member of the board of the Fine Arts Department of the People's Commissariat of Public Education, and from 1920 was a member of the Institute of Artistic Culture. In 1924-1925 she was Professor of the Textile Department of the Higher State Technical Art Studios.

She designed costumes for the farce *The Death of Tarelkin* by A. Sukhovo-Kobylin at the Meierkhold Theater in 1922. From the end of the 1920s she designed books, magazines, albums, and posters, often with her husband A. Rodchenko. In 1945-1946 she was on the staff of the magazine *Sovetskaia zhenshchina* (Soviet Woman).

67.
The notebook is in the possession of the artist's daughter, V. A. Rodchenko.

68.
Ibid.

be acceptable."[67] The artists were reproached for drawing "with the help of compasses and a ruler, which means they cannot draw" and "their drawings, like a spring, are all tied together and built on mathematics."[68]

There was some truth in this criticism: charmed by the design itself and by the possibilities of combinations of geometrical forms and colors, the designers divorced, as it were, the textile design from the texture of the fabric, with the result that the ponderous design rhythms did not work well with the flimsy, light calico. They were aware of it themselves. One such drawing Stepanova wittily called "construction of a bridge." After six months' work at the factory, however, the artists mastered the laws of textile. They were gradually recognized by the members of the factory's art council, as well as by the consumers, who discovered for themselves the unexpected beauty of bright, dynamic geometric patterns. Critics of those years finally acknowledged the significance of Stepanova's and Popova's efforts: "Marquisette and calicos have not only become artistically competent but have risen to the level of an uncommon art in this uncommon epoch and have begun conveying in endless streams to the cities of our immense republic the saturated colors and wonderful decoration of the art of today."[69]

69.
D. Aranovich, "Pervaia sitsenabivnaia fabrika v Moskve" in *Iskusstvo odevatsia*, 1928, no. 1, p. 11.

195

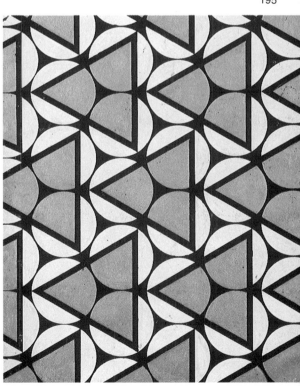

193

194

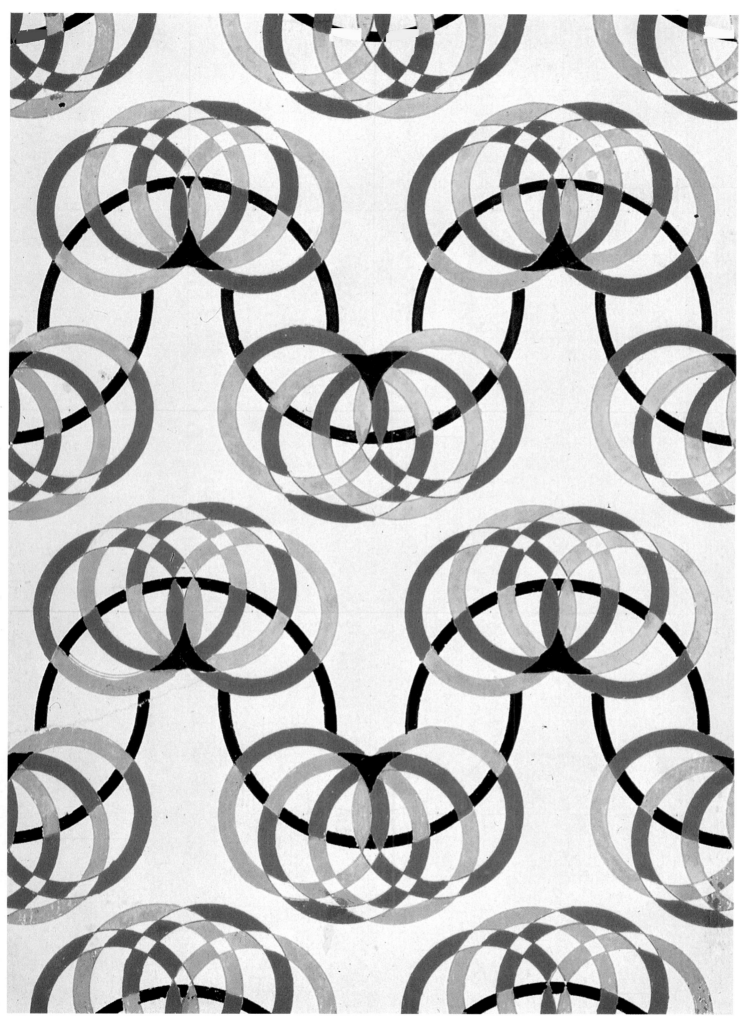

196

148

196, 197
V. Stepanova. Fabric designs.
1924.

198

199

198, 199

V. Stepanova. Sketches of sports uniforms. 1924. Varvara Stepanova took a great interest in designing sport uniforms, in which she applied her ideas of simple, comfortable clothing.

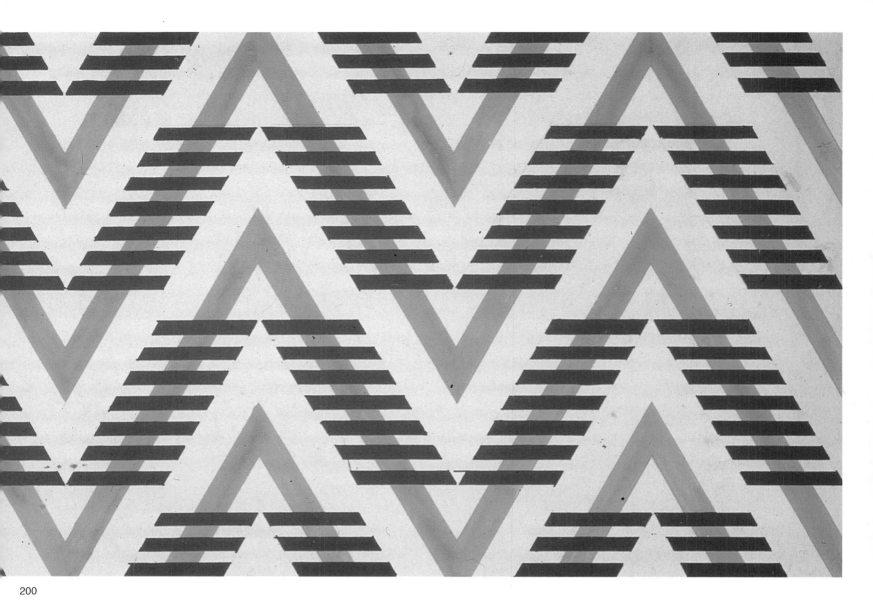

200

201

200

V. Stepanova. Fabric design. 1924.

201

V. Stepanova. Sketch of a sports
uniform. 1924.

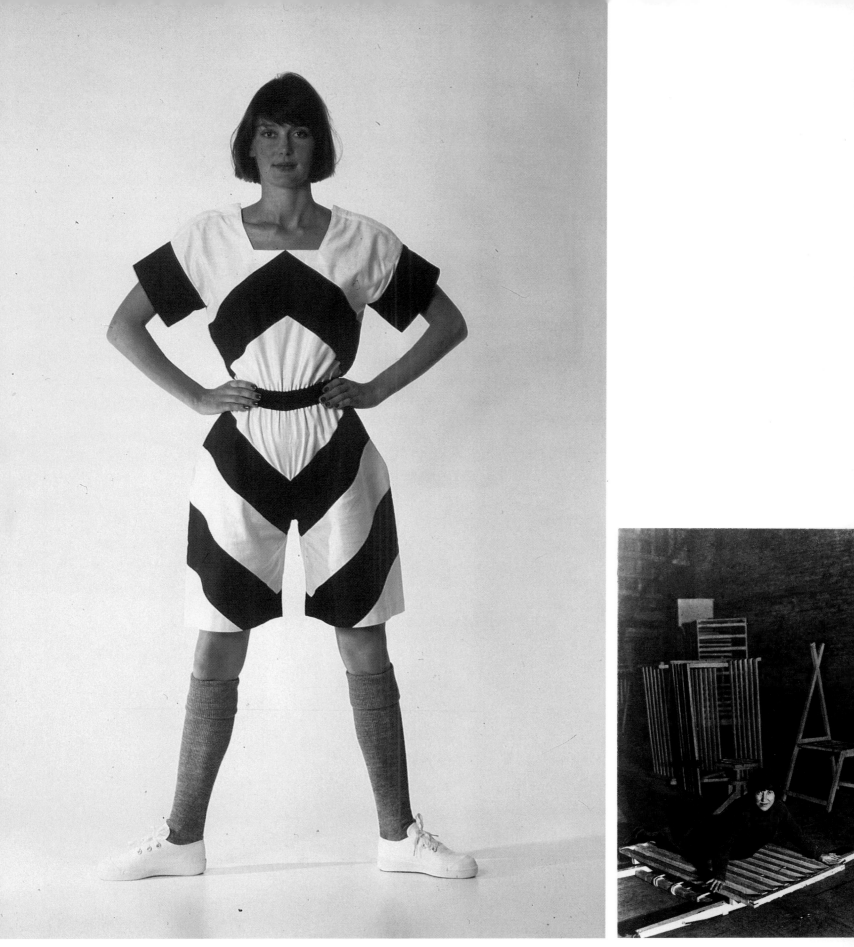

202

202

A sports uniform after a 1924 sketch by Stepanova. Reconstruction by E. Khudiakova. 1985.

203

Varvara Stepanova assembling the set for *The Death of Tarelkin* produced by V. Meierkhold after A. Sukhovo-Kobylin's play in 1922. Sketches of the costumes were also by Stepanova.

Although in their views, goals and methodology Stepanova and Popova resembled each other, in their practical textile and costume design they were quite different. Popova's textile geometrics are light and graceful, with softer graphic rhythms and more half-tones. They impart a sort of airiness to her sketches and allow her design to integrate easily with the ground. The range of Popova's motifs for calico is extensive, from simple repeated elements to composite crossing or superimposed circles and lattices. The designer's sketches show that she was mindful of the ultimate purpose of a textile design. She had had some hands-on experience, for by 1917, already keen on suprematist painting, she tried to find practical ways to apply her innovations. That led her to the *artel* (association) of expert folk embroiderers in the village of Verbovka in the Ukraine. By that time the *artel* was executing, from avant-garde artists' sketches, small embroidery-collages in the suprematist style, with carefully elaborated color schemes.

Popova joined this group of artists, enjoying the creation of these miniature collages, which were copies of her large paintings. The experience served as a preparatory stage for the artist's subsequent work in the textile industry, and expanded her knowledge of texture and fabric.

Stepanova's textile designs are somewhat different — they are more graphic and symbolic, emphasizing metaphor and rhythm. Prevalent in her early works were combinations of simple geometric shapes: triangles, squares, circles, and rectangles. Later she revealed more complexity in her decoration. The artist was concerned with the problems of proportion, dimension, the depth of the pattern, and its many layers superposed on the ground.

Like all constructivists, the artists were against continuity in art, proposing that the forms of the old costume be discarded and replaced by new ones. The constructivists saw new forms in *prozodezhda* (the worker's clothes), and called it the "costume of today." *Prozodezhda* could consist of many types of professional clothing, but particularly sports clothes. Stepanova, having assumed the functions of a theorist of industrial art, wrote articles and reports on the subject, while Popova attempted to transform the textile department of VKhUTEMAS (Higher

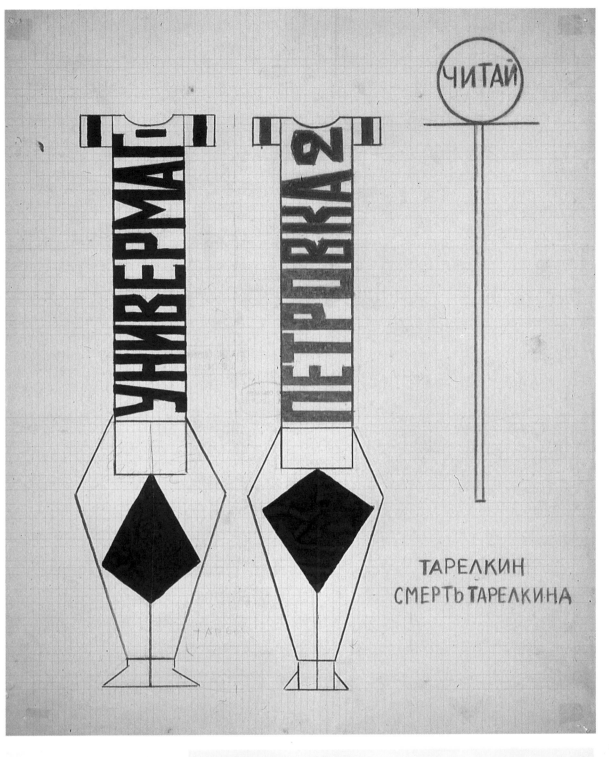

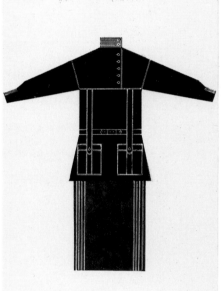

204-205

V. Stepanova. Sketches of costumes for the play *The Death of Tarelkin*. 1922. Stepanova's theater costumes were close to a uniform, or *prozodezhda*. She used the simplified geometrized scheme used by the constructivists. The style of costumes was in harmony with the innovative production of the play.

206

V. Stepanova. Sketch of woman's *prozodezhda*. 1924.

206

204

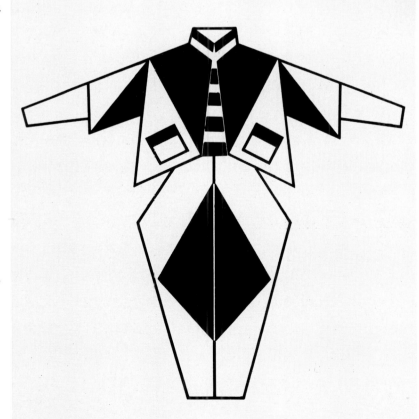

205

State Technical Art Studies) into a *prozodezhda* workshop.

Having studied in detail the manufacturing process for work clothes, Stepanova formulated a number of principles and outlined the stages of clothing construction from a clear differentiation of its functions and applying the system of cutting out and assembling to its practical use. "Two basic principles govern clothing today: comfort and expediency. There is no one single type of clothing, but rather specific clothing for specific functions. . . . It is not enough to design clothing, one must also produce it. *Prozodezhda* is individualized according to profession. Sports uniforms, for example, are characterized by a minimum of items; ease in putting on and wearing; a significance in the colors used to distinguish sportsmen and sport groups."[70]

70.
TsGAOR, f. 5721, op. 1, d. 1, p. 20.

In her innovative program Stepanova tried to foresee every detail in the process of clothing manufacture, stressing the garments' functionality and purpose. She attached special importance to construction, tailoring, and cut.

Following her guidelines, the constructivists worked out experimental samples of work clothes, some of whose elements became firmly established in mass production. Among them were comfortable overalls with

207

208

207, 208

V. Stepanova. Sketches of costumes for the play *Through the Red and the White Spectacles*. 1923.

plentiful and practical pockets and zippers. Stepanova herself designed clothes for surgeons, pilots, firemen, as well as uniform caps for the State Publishing House salesmen. Although she created a theory of work clothes design, Stepanova did not often apply it in her own work (apart from theater costume). The exceptions were a few everyday clothes of her own fabrics (usually designed for herself), and a few finished prototypes of work clothes.

One of the most important types of new costume for the constructivists were sports clothes, particularly team uniforms. Physical culture had acquired tremendous significance in the postrevolutionary decade. In designing a sports uniform, Stepanova declared: "All decorative and embellishing aspects should be done away with by the slogan 'comfort and utility for professional function.'"[71] Her sketches are simplified to a planar scheme consisting of geometrized elements: rectangles, squares, and more complicated shapes. And although the elimination of the "decorative aspect" was widely proclaimed in favor of utility, the constructivists (Stepanova above all), contradicting themselves, asserted that this type of clothing necessitated emblems and symbols that differentiated teams. No less essential for the sports uniform was its color, for during games held in big stadiums, the athletes' clothes alone could serve as a point of reference.

In contrast to Stepanova, Popova was less interested in designing sports uniforms than lightweight women's dresses made of printed fabrics of her own design. These dresses were unusual for the constructivist style: fashionable, much more bourgeois than proletarian, and clearly not destined for the masses. The elongated dress was often bloused at the waist or slightly below, the skirt had soft pleats or gathers, and collars and necklines were unusually shaped. Popova liked spectacular wide and soft fabric belts, and was particularly interested in the details and shape of the sleeves and cuffs.

The artist's favorite type of costume was an ensemble consisting of a long flowing blouse with a loose pleated skirt. She paid special attention to the appropriateness of a printed design for the shape of the dress. Side by side with a calico textile design could often be found the

71.
Varst (penname of V. Stepanova), "Kostium segodniashnego dnia-prozodezhda," *Lef*, 1923, no. 2, p. 65.

209
V. Stepanova. Sketch of a woman's costume. 1924.

210, 211
C. Stepanova. Sketch of a dress. 1924. A dress made after this sketch. Reconstruction by E. Khudiakova. 1985.

212
A. Rodchenko. A nonobjective composition. 1918.

213
Alexandr Rodchenko in a suit made from his sketch by his wife, the artist Varvara Stepanova. 1922.

214-215
A. Rodchenko. Sketches of costumes for the play *We* by A. Gan. 1921. The play was never produced.

212

Alexandr Rodchenko (1891-1956)

Alexandr Mikhailovich Rodchenko was born in St. Petersburg. He studied at the art school in Kazan under N. Feshin (1910-1913). In 1914-1916 he was a student of the Stroganov Industrial Art School in Moscow. In 1916 he participated in the Magazine exhibition, and two years later was a member of the board of the Fine Arts Department of the People's Commissariat of Public Education. In 1920-1930, he was one of the organizers and then head of the production

213

department of the Higher State Technical Art Institute — Higher State Technical Art Studios. From 1920 he was a member and, after 1921, chairman of the Institute of Artistic Culture.

Rodchenko was an organizer and participant in the exhibition held during the Third Congress of Comintern in 1920. In 1925 he participated in the international exhibition of decorative arts in Paris (and received four Silver Medals). His works were: a project for a workers' club furnishings, architecture, furniture, and costumes.

In 1918 he began to design costumes and settings for plays staged at the Meierkhold theater. After the early 1930s he worked in photography, poster and industrial design, and designed books and magazines. In 1927-1930 he worked in the cinema. Rodchenko participated in many exhibitions in the USSR and abroad.

artist's sketch of a dress from the same fabric. She tried to match decoration to the peculiarities of the dress's construction, to balance proportion and scale, and to harmonize the whole with the human figure. Aware that the bright and active constructivist design could easily annihilate the garment's shape, Popova resorted to "remnant" fabrics, in which a bodice remained white and unpatterned next to a decorated skirt, or a simple white skirt was paired with an ornamented bodice. Mixing plain and patterned surfaces was a typical feature of Popova's designs.

Sometimes, to accentuate the proportions of the dress, she merely edged its various parts, piping the cuffs of the sleeves, the hemline of the jacket, skirt, and collar. Popova's sketches show, as a rule, that she preferred simple decoration.

A noteworthy contribution to the history of the constructivist movement was made by Alexandr Rodchenko.

216, 217

A. Rodchenko. Fabric designs. 1924. In creating geometric ornaments, the constructivists combatted plant patterns which, in their opinion, were terribly "bourgeois." Rodchenko was astonished, however, when during his visit to capitalist France in 1925, he saw in Paris department stores fabrics with geometric designs produced on a mass scale. He then realized that ornament did not always develop according to the laws of class struggle. In his innovative searches, Rodchenko, with the help of simple instruments, anticipated computer graphics.

218

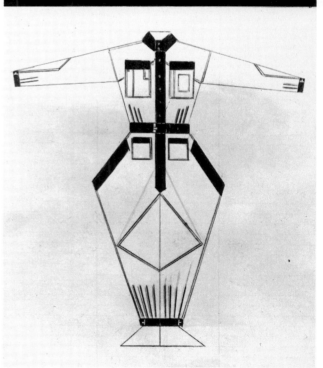

ЧЛЕН ПРОФСОЮЗА
ПЕРВЫМ
ПОЙДЕТ
В
РАБФАК
и ВУЗЫ

ПРОФСОЮЗНЫЙ
ЧЛЕНСКИЙ
БИЛЕТ

219

218, 220, 221

Alexandr Rodchenko in a wool suit
trimmed with leather, of his own
design. Beside it is the sketch of
the suit and its variation. 1922.

219

A. Rodchenko. *A Trade Union
Member Will Be the First to Enter
the Workers' Faculty and Higher
Schools.* Poster. 1925.

An artist of versatile talent, he was on the editorial board of the magazine *Lef* and at the same time enthusiastically drafted and put into practice projects for work clothes. There is the widely known Rodchenko work suit or, to be more precise, everyday overalls — perfectly rational and simple in construction (Rodchenko's sketch of them closely resembles Stepanova's). They were made of wool edged with a broad band of leather on the stand-up collar, pocket and cuffs. Besides buttons, metal buckles were used for closures. The artist was very fond of these overalls and wore them often, affirming and advertising his own and his fellow constructivists' art.

In accordance with the spirit of this romantic time, Rodchenko applied his talent to many fields of art: he designed posters, worked in advertising, designed residential and public building interiors (his famous "workers' club," for instance), made ensembles of furniture and architecture.[72] He was interested in painting, and was an excellent photographer.

72.
The project was shown at the International Exhibition in Paris in 1925.

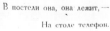

222

223

224

222, 223
A. Rodchenko. Illustrations for V. Maiakovsky's poem *About This*. 1923.

224
Gustav Klutsis. *For the Unity of Workers and Sportsmen of all Countries!* Poster. 1923.

225

226

225

A. Rodchenko. Design of a
newsstand. 1919.

226

A scene from the play *The Death
of Tarelkin*, with stage design by V.
Stepanova. 1922. ''The future is
our only aim'' says the slogan on
Rodchenko's design of a
newsstand. Even when creating
costumes for a 19th-century play,
Stepanova, too, was thinking of
the future.

But it was with especially loving care that he created designs for theater performances. In 1925 Rodchenko helped to stage V. Maiakovsky's comedy *The Bedbug* at the Revolution Theater. The album of costume sketches contains drawings and descriptions of costumes of every character in the play, and reveals quite a few innovative finds: in individual articles of costume (the above-mentioned overalls); in details (convenient zip-fasteners); and finally, in the reduction of the volume of clothes to make them more practical.[73]

When he was asked to design the scenery and costumes for the play *Inga* by A. Glebov — dealing with a new persona in Soviet psychology, the builder of the socialist society — Rodchenko designed clever and practical forms of folding wooden furniture which were simple to the point of being radical in their minimal use of space. Just as austere and utilitarian were the costumes of the characters in the play.

73.
The album with the sketches is owned by the artist's daughter, V. A. Rodchenko.

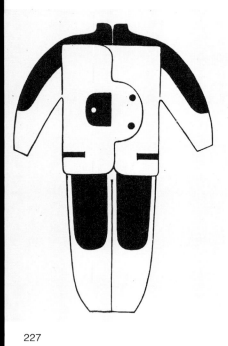

227

228

229

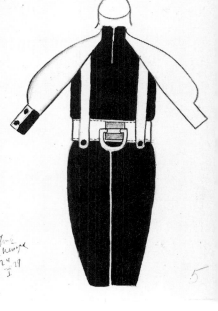

230

227-230

A. Rodchenko. Sketches of costumes for V. Maiakovsky's play *The Bedbug* and a costume made from one of the sketches. 1929. Maiakovsky's play is based on the contrast between the philistine life of the 1920s and life in the beautiful "morrow." Meierkhold asked realist artists, like Kukrynisky, to design the stage for contemporary scenes, and the constructivist Rodchenko to make the stage design for the scenes taking place in the future.

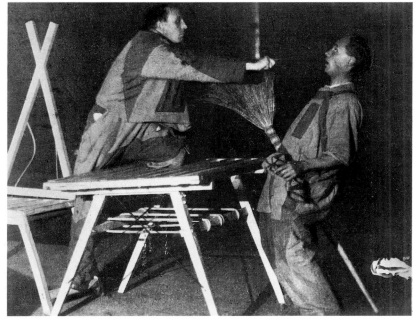

231

231-233
Scenes from *The Death of Tarelkin*, with stage design by V. Stepanova. 1922.

234
A scene from the play *Through the Red and the White Spectacles*, with stage design by Stepanova. 1923. Stylized costumes of a worker and a peasant.

235-237
A. Rodchenko. Sketches of costumes for A. Glebov's play *Inga* staged at the Revolution Theater in Moscow in 1929.

234

232

233

238-241
Transforming man by changing his way of life was the leading idea of the constructivists. It was fervently championed by Vladimir Tatlin. Working at the material culture section of the Science Central Administrative Board, Tatlin created a coat and a suit of a "new type," which "did not hamper movement, was hygienic" and practical. The coat consisted of three pieces: a waterproof outside and two linings. The flannel lining was used in autumn

While appreciating Rodchenko's desire to design a practical, expedient form of costume, one cannot help but notice that both his costruction and cutting obey the logic of an abstractly geometrized scheme with easily discernible elements of cubistic painting. It is impossible to find a functional justification for his intricate division of the designs into triangles, in the zigzag lines of the lapel, and in the placement and overabundance of buttons. For the sake of eccentricity, the artist distorted the proportions of his suits, sometimes excessively stretching and lengthening them.

The material culture section (OMK) under the Central Administrative Board for Science was engaged at that time in designing everyday, "average" clothes. It was with this section that Vladimir Tatlin made his designs. Most interesting among them was a clever jacket that could be transformed from a winter into a summer garment: one could exchange the autumn lining made of flannel for the winter one made of fur. Moreover, the jacket had sections that could be replaced when worn out. Tatlin applied the same versatility to a summer suit: the artist was often photographed in the famous jacket that resulted from this experiment. He himself made the patterns and reproduced them in magazines. He was also the creator of comfortable chairs and armchairs with flexible metal frames and practical tableware designs. Like most of his artist contemporaries, he saw the human environment as a multifaceted complex compilation of simple designs.

235

236

237

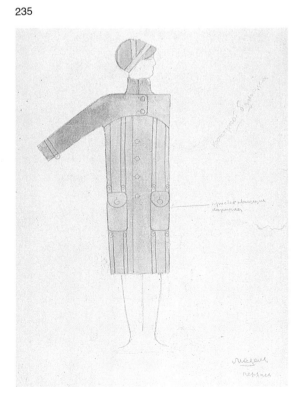
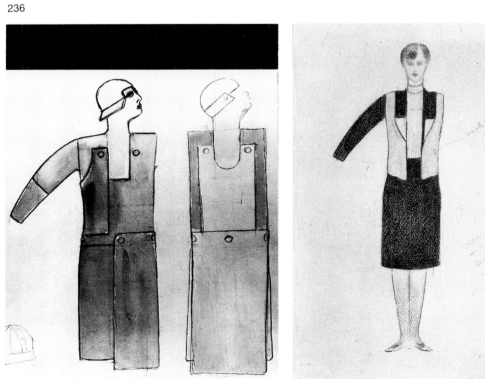

238 240
239 241

and the fur lining in winter. Each piece could be replaced when it wore out. Tatlin wore and advertised his clothes, and was often photographed in them. In the photomontage "The New Way of Life," Tatlin shows that the new form of clothing wipes out all the achievements of the past. Neither the tuxedo nor the dinner jacket have any place in the present or in the future. Alongside are Tatlin's designs of women's and men's garments of the early 1920s. On the page from the Moscow City Council book published in 1934 for the 17th Congress of the Communist Party of the Soviet Union (Bolsheviks) we see Tatlin, the "inventor in the field of garment industry" next to his aircraft.

The Vesnin brothers, Alexandr and Viktor, who created costumes for *The Man Who Was Thursday* by G. K. Chesterton, and a number of other plays, are also well-known designers of this period. Kazimir Malevich was celebrated for his sketches of "suprematist textiles" and "suprematist dress."

Sketches of costumes for the plays staged in the 1920s were made by I. Nivinsky, V. and G. Stenberg, G. Klutsis, N. Akimov, N. Anzimova, N. Altman, and many other talented artists.

242

243

242

N. Udaltsova. Fabric design. Early 1920s.

243

N. Udaltsova. Embroidery design. Early 1920s.

244

G. Klutsis. Sketch of miner's work clothes. 1922.

245

N. Udaltsova. Fabric design. Early 1920s.

245

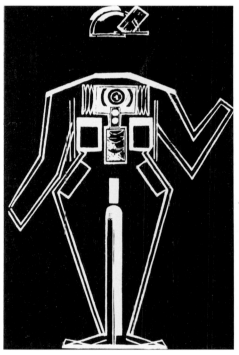

244

246

G. Miller. Sketch of a coal miner's work clothes. 1924. Sharing the ideas of Malevich in the pre-revolutionary years, Nadezhda Udaltsova in the 1920s came close to the constructivists' circle. With Rodchenko, Stepanova, and Popova, she took part in the discussions, made holiday decorations and designed clothes. Her fabric designs reveal her powerful pictorial gift. However, her love of painting eventually prevailed.

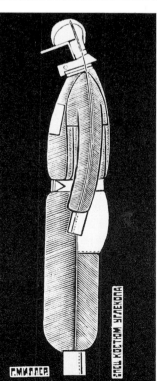

246

247-249

A. Vesnin. Sketches of costumes for the play *The Man Who Was Thursday* based on G. K. Cherterton's novel. 1922-1923. The production of the play by Alexandr Tairov at the Chamber Theater in Moscow, with costume and stage design by Vesnin, was the event of the season. The staging was made in the best (although young) constructivist traditions; its asymmetry was akin to that of the architectural forms of the Palace of Labor, on which Vesnin was working with his brothers. Vesnin's costume designs differed from those of other constructivists. Popova, Stepanova, and Rodchenko all interpreted costume as a geometrized scheme. Vesnin offered individual garments for each character in an intensely modern key: the dress and costumes with a low waist, tapered skirt, wide cuffs, and high collars.

250

O. Rozanova. Sketch of a bag. 1917.

248

247

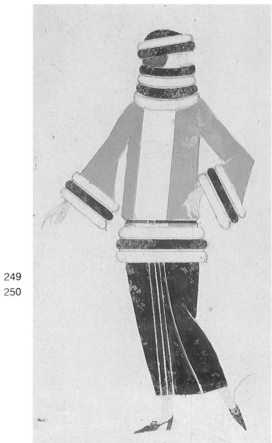

249
250

СПИ Ч КИН

251

N. Aizenberg. Sketch of a costume
for Spichkin in a performance of
Blue Blouse. 1920s.

Clothing Design in the Late 1920s

It had probably became clear by the mid-1920s that the impetuous period of enthusiasm and unquestioning belief in the radical transformation of culture was nearing its end. Reality had a sobering effect on the romantics who had been anticipating a swift actualization of the grandiose revolutionary projects to transform Soviet life. Although the aims of the program to improve culture did not change, the radicalism and extremism of the revolutionary decade eventually proved impracticable. This view had been expressed by Lenin in 1921: "Borne along on the wave of excitement, rousing first the political enthusiasm and then the military enthusiasm of the people, we expected to accomplish economic tasks just as great as the political and military tasks we had accomplished by relying directly on this enthusiasm. We expected — or perhaps it would be truer to say that we presumed, without having given it adequate consideration — to be able to organize state production and distribution of products on communist lines in a small-peasant country directly, as ordered by the proletarian state. Experience has proved that we were wrong."[74]

Lenin's words also explain why the first Soviet artists' optimistic efforts

74.
N. I. Lenin, "Fourth Anniversary of the October Revolution," *Collected Works*. Progress Publishers, Moscow, vol. 33, p. 58.

252

252

N. Aizenberg. Sketch of costumes for a show based on V. Maiakovsky's poems. 1925. The costume of the theatrical character parodies the clothes of a rogue and idler. He has on his head a modish, unusual-looking cap, and wears a sporty football jersey with an open neck. The others are leftovers from the past: soldier's riding-breeches and puttees. Another costume sketch suggests a uniform for tram conductors.

253

253-257

N. Aizenberg. Sketches of
costumes for the *Blue Blouse*
productions. 1920s.
The 1920s were a high point for
professional theater, which opened
its doors to the new spectator.
Amateur companies, too, were
springing up everywhere. The
Blue Blouse was the brotherhood
of non-professional actors. Initially

the *Blue Blouses*, as is clear from
the name, had no costumes, but
simply put on a blue sateen shirt,
entered the stage and enacted
topical plays that they themselves
composed. Satire is perceptible in
the costumes of the woman
official, the woman machine-
gunner, the conscript, the
cavalryman, and the artilleryman.

in clothing production failed. The ideal of the costume designers' contacts with industrial production, correct in principle, was not realized, owing to the shortage of skilled designers, technologists, and pattern makers. There were not enough capable, experienced garment industry specialists, and the level of industrial production was too low.

This gap between potential and realization applies, above all, to the work of Lamanova. This artist, who was convinced of the feasibility of her program, was compelled to confine herself to "laboratory" experiments or to serve individual customers. The talented costume designers, who had eagerly believed in the new forms of Soviet costume, found themselves by the end of the decade working with handicraft organizations or fashion workshops. Lamanova transferred her activities to exporting clothes and to the theater; Mukhina, although she remained a member of clothing art councils and of the clothing section of the State

255 256 257

Academy of Artistic Sciences, practically ceased to work in this domain. Pribylskaia, Stepanova and other artists created clothing designs at the Handicraft Export. (Stepanova, after the sudden death of Popova, left the factory workshop in 1924 because she refused, on principle, the inclusion of plant motifs in her textile sketches, thereby upholding her position as an innovative constructivist.)

Soon after its opening, the Atelier of Fashions ceased to address the mass-production client and began catering exclusively to individual customers, particularly rich businessmen. As noted by the critic F. Roginskaia, having changed its "clientele," the Atelier of Fashions abandoned the independent road in favour of Western fashion. Neither the Atelier of Fashions nor the *Lef* artists had ever been closely in touch with mass garment production.

In an attempt to remain faithful to their principles of simple clothing

258

for the masses, many artists — including Lamanova, Stepanova, and Pribylskaia — pinned their hopes on the Moscow Handicrafts Export, which declared its devotion to the "mass consumer." In her article "The Problems of Costume," Roginskaia examined in detail the Moscow Handicrafts Export activities, seeing in this organization a means for carrying out the plans of mass production of modern garments.[75] She analyzed the aims and tasks of the organization, which tried, in her words, to work out "two types of clothing for mass consumption."[76] The first type was the clothing whose decorative elements (often embroidered towels and lace) were executed in the peasant *artels* of Kaluga, Novgorod, Tula and other towns. The second type she categorized as "pure

75.
Sovetskoie iskusstvo, 1926, no. 7, pp. 63-67.

76.
Quotations here and elsewhere are from F. Roginskaia's article "Problemy kostiuma" in *Sovetskoie iskusstvo*, 1926, no. 7, pp. 63-67.

260

259

ВЫКРОЙКА КОСТЮМА ЧАСТУШЕЧНИЦЫ

261

258

N. Aizenberg. Sketch of a sports outfit for *Blue Blouse*. 1920s.

259

N. Aizenberg. Pattern of a costume for the *Blue Blouse chastooshka* singer. 1920s. (Chastooshka is a two-line or four-line or folk verse, usually humorous and topical, sung in a lively manner.)

260-262

Blue Blouse performances. 1920s. *Blue Blouse* companies of actors were created at the institutes and at communal residential houses. V. Shalamov writes that there were about 500 throughout the country. *Blue Blouse* plays recounted contemporary events, efforts to build a new life, the world of the future, and the struggle against the past. The shows were something of a living newspaper with feature stories, leading articles and satires.

262

263

265

264

266

263-266

A. Petritsky. Sketches of costumes

N. Akimov. Sketch of a woman's costume for the play *Evgraf the Adventurer*. 1926.

267

268

N. Altman. Sketch of a woman's costume for the play *Comrade Shindel.* 1926. A Young Communist League member of the 1920s is approvingly portrayed by Altman in felt boots and a jacket made out of sailor's pea jacket.

270

269-272

Blue Blouse performances. 1920s. *Blue Blouse* revues dealt with everything — the defense industry, construction work, the miracles of chemistry, and the joy of flying in a plane. Lenin's dictum ''Communism is a system of civilized cooperators'' was demonstrated by the *Blue Blouses*. The blue blouses are discernible on the photograph on the right. Of the same cut, wide on the bottom and with gathers under the yoke, the blouses resembled the Tolstoy-style shirts that were so popular at the turn of the century.

urban interpretation," for which the constructivists Stepanova, Rod-chenko, and Lavinsky created an original "decoration of a geometric style." Whole fragments or bands of a geometric ornamental motif were sewn onto the dress like an appliqué. Both types of costume could serve as models and patterns for a self-taught dressmaker. The main function of the Moscow Handicrafts Export, however, was to sell one-of-a-kind specimens of handcrafted clothing abroad to popularize traditionally Russian forms and ornamentation of costume at international exhibitions, and, of course, to support the handicraft industry. So there was serious doubt that this association could solve the problem of industrial production. In fact, it would require more than the resolution of technological and organizational problems; it would require a transformation of the cultural level of the country as a whole. Lenin repeatedly said that "a cultural problem cannot be solved as quickly as political and military problems. . . . It is possible to obtain victory in war in a few months. But it is impossible to achieve a cultural victory in such a short time. By its very nature it requires a longer period; and we must adapt ourselves to this longer period, plan our work accordingly, and display the maximum of perseverance, persistence and method."[77]

In the art of costume, tradition plays a major role. It will be recalled that France, the center of world fashion, has its cultural traditions rooted deep in the Middle Ages. Many centuries' evolution of the art of dressing have produced modern French clothing, and made French

77.
V. I. Lenin, "Report to the Second All-Russian Congress of Political Education Departments," 17 October 1921. *Collected Works*, Progress Publishers, Moscow, vol. 33, pp. 78-79.

273-276

The Stenberg brothers. Sketches
of costumes for S. Semenov's play
Natalia Tarpova, 1929. The refined
color sketches lack the strict
geometrization of the figure that is
found in the constructivists'
theater costumes, although their
designers were the Stenberg
brothers, the famous
constructivists who proclaimed this
art in 1922 and produced spatial
compositions typical of the genre.
Vladimir and Georgii Stenberg
cooperated closely with the
Moscow Chamber Theater from
1922 to 1931, and even joined it in
its tours abroad. The sketches of
women's evening and everyday
dresses, despite being extremely
stylized, show the new fashion
tendencies of the late 1920s.
There is a return to femininity:
skirts are tight-fitting and flared,
cut on the bias, with a naturally
placed waist. Evening dresses are
décolleté. Outer clothing, after a
long predominance of the
diamond-shaped silhouette,
returns to the rectangle.

277

277
S. Strusevich. *Lamps*, cotton print.
Late 1920s.

278
Sergei Burylin. *Russian Fairy Tale*,
cotton print. Late 1920s.

279
Mariia Anufrieva. *Industrial*, cotton
print. Late 1920s.

280

278

279

280
Konstantin Yuon. *Hammer and
Sickle*, fabric design. 1923.
At the close of the 1920s, a new
generation of artists, graduates of
VKhUTEMAS-VKhUTEIN, began
to work in the textile industry.
Although they were disciples of
the constructivists, they did not
adhere to their belief in fabrics'
geometric ornamentation.
They announced: "We are not
afraid of the so-called slavish
dependence on painting. The
problems facing textile artists
in no way differ from those of
painters or illustrators." Textiles
featured light bulbs to champion
electrification; gears for
industrialization. These ideas
tempted even traditional textile
designers like Sergei Burylin, who
had worked at a factory for almost
half a century. He introduced into
his designs themes imitating Ivan
Bilibin's illustrations of Russian
fairy tales.

designers the world's best.

Soviet clothes design, on the other hand, was practically devoid of tradition: its beginnings coincided with the October Revolution, and more realistically, the early 1930s, when the Moscow House of Clothing Design opened.

By the end of the 1920s, however, some changes were taking place in the garment industry. Some of the old textile and garment enterprises were being rebuilt, and they acquired specialized equipment and machinery capable of producing goods in large quantities. These were, nevertheless, only the first steps in overhauling the country's textile industry. From an editorial in the new magazine *Shveinaia promyshlennost* (The Garment Industry) we learn that by the beginning of the 1930s only 30 percent of work at garment factories was mechanized, and that, as usual, there was an acute shortage of machines and factories.[78]

78.
"O tekhnicheskoi rekonstruktsii shveinoi promyshlennosti" in *Shveinaia promyshlennost*, 1931, no. 8, p. 8.

The late 1920s were marked by heated discussion on the problems of mass producing the new clothing and textile designs. After flaring up like bright stars, Popova and Stepanova's novel ideas for fabrics soon faded without finding any support in industry. The same fate awaited the geometric designs created in the late 1920s by L. Maiakovskaia at the Trekhgornaia Textile Mill. Her textile designs, intended for soft velvet, ingeniously interpreted various geometric shapes — concentric circles, acute triangles and broken lines — which acquired numerous color effects thanks to the velvet texture: a glimmering depth, changing tonal combinations, and an impressive richness. The artist's designs were always imposed on a dark ground and consisted of fine contour lines or a diffuse painterly planar pattern, the pile of the velvet tending to subdue and smooth the transitions, making the outlines appear to melt into one another. Maiakovskaia's experiments, however, were unique, and no one intended to repeat them or much less use them in quantity production.

Nevertheless, the artist accomplished her task brilliantly. She invented a modified airbrush for spray painting, using it to apply her decoration to velvet. Despite their experimental nature, Maiakovskaia's designs

282

281
Liudmila Maiakovskaia. Design for velvet. Late 1920s.

282
Liudmila Maiakovskaia. *Circles*, design for velvet. Late 1920s.

283
Maiakovskaia at the Tekhgornaia Textile Mill. Late 1920s. In the late 1920s, the popularity of geometric design declined, but a few artists continued to explore its possibilities. One of them was Liudmila Maiakovskaia, the elder sister of Vladimir Maiakovsky. Maiakovskaia's designs of circles, triangles and interrupted lines intended for velvet acquired, thanks to the fabric's texture, numerous color effects: glimmering depth, changing tonal combinations, and impressive richness.

281

283

284

Babashev. *Construction Site*,
cotton print. Late 1920s.

285

Anonymous designer. *Geometric*,
cotton print. Mid-1920s.

286

Anonymous designer. *Geometric*,
cotton print. Mid-1920s.

287

S. Buntsis. *Forge*, cotton print.
1931. The supporters of textiles'
function as propaganda spoke at
meetings and published their
articles in newspapers and
magazines. They showed thematic
designs to the public at the Soviet
Textiles in Everyday Life exhibition
in Moscow in 1928. The range of
themes used in fabric design
included construction and factory
work, and the activities of the
armed forces. Fabrics with
geometric paterns coexisted at
this time with propaganda textiles.

influenced a line of industrial designs printed on soft, loose-weave fustian.

Toward the end of the 1920s, the low quality of industrially produced fabrics, the lack of interest in aesthetics by those in factory laboratories, and the tendency to give in to the consumer's old-fashioned tastes, presented a barrier to the development of design in industrial production. Nor was the problem confined to textile manufacture, but carried over into other branches of industrial art as well.

A large-scale campaign was begun against low-grade fabrics and clothes, and became part of the general protest against the low level of culture in everyday life and the struggle against tastelessness and vulgarity.

By that time the first group of professional fabric and fashion artists were graduating from the secondary special training schools, and many of them went on to head the campaign for a new vocabulary of fabric design, more in tune with the contemporary tasks facing the arts. Those artists who had graduated from the textile department at VKhUTEIN took as their catch-phrase "the creation of new thematic fabric designs," showing the first examples of their work in 1928 at the Soviet Textiles in Everyday Life exhibition. The section in which their works were on display was called Specific Patterns of the New Searches. Among the pioneers

of this trend were Raitser, Lekhtman, Chachkhiani, Anufrieva, and Kotov.

The core of the young people's program was presented in the press and at meetings at VKhUTEIN. According to them, fabric design was faced with the same problems as painting: it had to both reflect life, and try to change it for the better. N. Poluektova, a supporter of "theme" textiles, wrote: "We are not afraid of slavish dependence on painting . . . the problems facing textile artists in no way differ from those that painters or illustrators have to deal with."[79]

The list of "themes" to be used in fabric design reflected the important issues of the day: construction, electrification, accomplishments in culture and science, sport, and the life of the Komsomol and Young Pioneers organizations.

The design of thematic patterns for industrial production was a complicated and interesting phenomenon, and marked one of the most creatively rich periods in the history of Soviet textile art. As a matter of fact, it was not all that new. Thematic motifs had been used for centuries in folk embroidery, fabric printing, carpets, and ceramics. Faced with the challenge of commemorating contemporary events, the most gifted of the new artists adapted current subject matter to conform to the laws governing the decorative organization of the flat surface as well as to

79.
N. Poluektova, "Za pravilnuiu pozitsiiu v tekstilnom risunke" in *Za proletarskoe iskusstvo*, 1932, no. 7-8, p. 25.

288

289

288

Bors Kustodiev. *The City (Provides) Textiles, the Countryside Bread*, sketch of a poster. 1925.

289

N. Vasileva. *The New Countryside*, cotton print. 1930.

290

Anonymous designer. *Agriculture*, cotton print. 1930.

291

L. Silich. *Reapers*, cotton print. Late 1920s. Textiles of the period of forced agricultural collectivization. The main buyers of fabrics in an agrarian country are the peasants. But a peasant woman who has just led her only cow to the commonly-owned herd is hardly likely to wear a dress featuring an enormous tractor. Bright, multicolored propaganda fabrics did not reach the villages, as they were often printed in small quantities, and many were produced only for exhibitions. Two- or three-colored fabrics were often mass-produced, as they were cheaper to manufacture. A brilliant example is Silich's work, which though done in the old picot technique, has an unusually modern appeal.

290
291

292
Anonymous designer. *The Red Navy*, cotton print. Late 1920s.

293
Anonymous designer. *Soviet Aviation*, cotton print. 1932.

294
Anonymous designer. *Dirigible*, cotton print. Late 1920s.

292
293

294

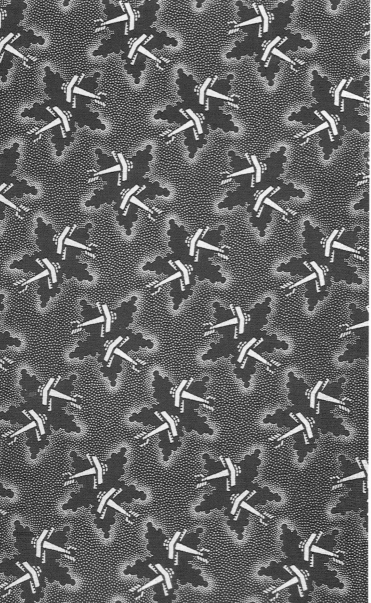

the technology of industrial production. The basic repeated motif was schematized, whether it was an emblem like the hammer and sickle, or an image of a factory, tractor, or human figure. Repeated regularly over the fabric's surface, the motif became a flat, graphic pattern, and the effect was heightened by the use of either monochrome or a limited palette of primary colors. Particularly effective were patterns composed of small repeat motifs outlined in fine contours, suitable for the light cotton prints, crêpes, and voiles so popular in the 1930s.

One of the most talented artists to design thematic fabrics was S. Burylin, who worked at the Bolshaia Ivanovskaia Textile Mill. His designs, such as "Industrial," "Tractors," and "Factory," are distinguished by their individuality and imagination, and their thoroughly textile-oriented approach to design. Despite the apparent difficulties inherent in adapting a subject for use in fabrics, Burylin could transform any thematic motif with ease. His "Tractor" print (early 1930s) is an example, on the one hand, of *agittema* ("agit-theme") and, on the other hand, of a creative interpretation of textile ornament. The repeated tractor motifs seem to actually move over the surface, but the movement is held in check by a series of textile "tricks" such as a generalized treatment of the ornament and a harmonization of the red patches with the striped ground. The fabric surface is covered uniformly with a balanced combination of geometric elements. The subject matter is "encoded," but on closer inspection can easily be recognized. "Encoding" the subject matter is a device used in the best of these fabrics, and can be seen in such designs as D. Preobrazhenskaia's "Industrial," O. Bogoslovskaia's "Construction," M. Nazarevkaia's "Electrification," and O. Griun's "Pioneers," to name only a few.

A distinct group of fabrics from the late 1920s and the early 1930s can be identified by the use of symbolic emblems like the hammer and sickle or five-pointed star in conjunction with letters and numbers. In a well-known printed cotton design by O. Griun, the hammer, sickle, and shafts of wheat are shown in large circles with a rising sun on a red ground dotted with tiny stars. This original decorative image became something of a "standard" for artists working in textile design. Thematic fabrics often incorporated words like "March 8," "USSR," and "KIM" (Communist Youth International). As a rule they were used in small repeat designs, so skillfully interwoven into the general composition that they are often difficult to discern. Similar methods and motifs were used on porcelain in that period.

Other thematic motifs included detailed and large-scale depiction of tractors, locomotives, and gears, entire scenes displaying the new face of the countryside, and portraits and book illustrations. These thematic textiles came close to performing the functions usually associated with painting, and although from a professional standpoint they followed the rules of textile design, the actual repeated motif itself was, in effect, a realistically executed picture, as in V. Lotonina's "The Navy" and V. Maslov's "Village Consumer Society."

The most zealous supporters of thematic textile design avoided using the word repeat-motif, referring to it instead as the picture or the subject, i.e., employing the terms of formal painting. In the press, it was not the textile design as such that was analyzed but the single unit: "Here you see before you a tractor column. . . . Looking at this design, you feel the power that emanates from the column . . . and you feel that life really can be remade in a new way, in the socialist way."[80] The author of these lines might well be describing a painting rather than a fabric whose constantly repeated element constitutes the overall pattern.

Usually, statics had no place in the composition of these designs — these fabrics were dynamic: locomotives raced, skiers sped, sportsmen swam, and airplanes flew. This introduction of movement complicated the task of fabric design, forcing the artist to think about ways to convey spatial depth, although this depth was often masked by schematizing techniques that kept it flat and decorative. The depiction of movement also had great symbolic relevance, for it conveyed the rhythm and speed of the epoch, the impetuousness of a young country in transition. However, such factors as the strange appearance of thematic textiles, the excessively categorical pronouncements made by artists striving to

80.
A. Kudriavtsev and I. Perepelitsyn, "O novom risunke v tekstile" in *Khlopchatobumazhnaia promyshlennost*, 1931, no. 8, p. 56.

295

N. Sokolov. *Airplanes*, cotton print. 1932.

296

L. Raitser. *Mechanization of the Workers' and Peasants' Red Army*, cotton print. 1933. Here fabrics with a large repeated design follow the laws of textile ornamentation, but the design is realistic. The task was complicated by the design's dynamism. Everything moves here: the planes, tanks and trucks full of soldiers, and a gear rises like the sun above all — the god of mechanization. Liia Raitser, a graduate of the Moscow VKhUTEIN, created this fabric not for dresses or curtains but for an exhibition. In 1933, the fabric was shown at the Workers' and Peasants' Red Army exhibition next to enormous paintings portraying the capture of Tsaritsyn and the storm of Perekop. Raitser's fabric is the swan song of "agitational" textiles. In the years of its appearance, the Council of People's Commissars decided upon the inadmissibility of such "inappropriate designs."

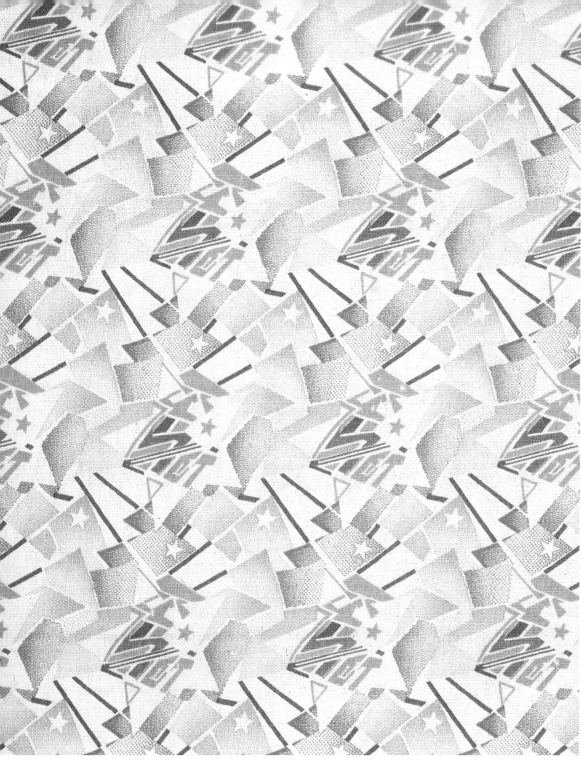

297

299
300
301
302

298

297
V. Losenva. *Fourteen Years of the October Revolution*, cotton print. 1931.

298
Anonymous designer. *USSR*, cotton print. Early 1930s.

299-302
O. Bogoslavskaia, E. Lapshin, and anonymous designer. Cotton prints. Early 1930s.

bring textile design closer to painting, and the tenuousness of some of the designs provoked stormy arguments in the press. The debate over the use of emblems in particular was indicative of the attempt to find a compromise between the thematic subject in fabric and its place in everyday life. A number of critics, among them A. Fedorov-Davydov and D. Arkin, felt that the use of emblems was the only acceptable way to express a theme in textiles.

In 1931, the newspaper *Golos tekstilia* (The Textile Voice) arranged a conference of specialists from various branches of the textile industry, during which it was pointed out that a pictorial approach to fabric design too often became an end in itself, as the designer was mindful of only one thing — how to equate the fabric with painting and how to popularize the socialist way of life. But the decisive blow at "thematic textiles" was struck by G. Ryklin in the satirical article "Tractor in Front, Grain Harvester Behind." Deriding the ideologists of industrial-thematic decoration, Ryklin said that "the tasks of political propaganda have been mechanically applied to textiles. Everything has its proper place! Let a picture hang in a picture gallery, let a poster mobilize for the accomplishment of urgent economic tasks . . . but let a dress or a suit remain a dress or a suit; there is no need to turn a Soviet citizen into a travelling picture gallery."[81]

In the same year of 1933, the Council of People's Commissars of the USSR adopted a resolution "On the Inadmissibility of the Goods Produced by Certain Fabric Enterprises Using Inferior and Inappropriate Designs."[82] Thus, instead of letting the trend die a natural, inevitable death, the authorities actually banned thematic motifs in fabrics. Soon after, the trend practically disappeared, to be resurrected only in the mid-1950s.

An important aspect of thematic textiles was that they represented the first stage in textile artists' effort to be creative in their work for industry. The artists saw themselves as members of a creative group engaged in an important collective endeavor. It was at that time that art studios began to be established at garment industry factories.

81.
G. Ryklin, "Speredi traktor-szadi kombain" in *Pravda*, 6 September 1933.

82.
"Postanovlenie ot 17 dekabria 1933 goda" in *Izvestia*, 18 December 1933.

303

303
D. Preobrazhenskaia. *KIM*, cotton
print. Early 1930s.

304
Anonymous designer. *Turksib*,
cotton print. 1927-1930.

305
Anonymous designer. *Production*,
cotton print. Early 1930s.

In the debates on Soviet mass-produced clothing and the relationship between fabric and form, the artists' view was upheld by a group of rather philistine sociologists, including "specialists" on costume (N. Poluektova, K. Mashurina, and R. Silich). They championed an ascetic proletarian costume, attacking Lamanova's principles of design, choosing from the artist's integral program to misinterpret her laws on the decoration of clothes. Their attacks were targeted at some dresses of handmade fabrics embellished with Lamanova's embroidery, which they labelled — as they labelled, for that matter, the artist's entire work — "applied decorativeness" and "formal skill of a handicraftsman." They also criticized Lamanova's principle "material determines form," alleging that she viewed clothes in isolation from a "social," i.e., class treatment of the subject. It should be noted, however, that one of the sociologists, Mashurina, based her own treatise precisely on the main points of Lamanova's program in her article on new clothes for the collective-farm village. Simultaneously, the presentation of new fashions was censured in maga-

zines, and the "Soviet image" was represented instead by socially active women in kerchiefs and militarized garments.

The vulgarizing attitudes of some sociologists became obvious during the discussion of one of the cardinal problems — how to co-ordinate the design of the fabric with the construction of the garment — and formed part of the campaign "For a Contemporary Thematic Design," which continued until 1933. Whereas some sociologists approved of identifying textile design with painting and an essentially independent function for textiles, the prominent art critic Fedorov-Davydov wrote: "Design is always one of the elements of artistic decoration, along with attaining a high quality of fabric; treating the fabric to increase its luster and density, giving it a shiny or matte finish; the coloring process, and all those aspects which are to be most closely associated with the functions of the garment, and which emphasize and clarify these functions. . . . The problem of textile will become part of the artistic decoration of the costume, both in terms of its design and in terms of its mass production."[83]

83.
A. Fedorov-Davydov, "Iskusstvo tekstilia" in *Sbornik: Izofront*. Moscow-Leningrad, 1931, pp. 82-90.

A common fault in textile design, art critic Arkin believed, was the attitude of the fabric designer who thought that his area of activity was unconnected to garment design: "As a rule fabric is chosen based solely on how it looks in its original uncut state. Absolutely no allowance is made for the transformation that occurs when the fabric is used. Textile designs have nothing in common with the forms in which the fabric is used."[84]

84.
D. Arkin, *"Iskusstvo veshchi,"* Moscow, 1929, p. 119.

Like textile design, the emphasis on dress design shifted at the close of the 1920s to the problems of realization of mass producing clothes. The activities of artists in the 1920s — the establishment of institutions dealing with clothing, the publication of specialized magazines and books, the disputes and competitions, participation in international exhibitions — attracted the attention of the public and created a favorable atmosphere for a serious, practical approach to the design of contemporary clothes, which soon was considered one of the most urgent tasks of cultural development.

306

Cover of the magazine *Iskusstvo
odevatsia*, 1928.

1. (Слева направо) Платье из сурового кустарного полотна, вышитое. Широкие полосы могут быть нашиты аппликацией из кумача или сатина. Такие же—кушак, продернутый через заметанные петли, и манжеты. Сумочка из той же материи, что и платье, с вышивкою теми же цветами. Полотна—4½ м. 2. Летнее платье из полотна, отделанное вышивками. Шарф может быть сделан из креп-де-шина или шиффона под цвет платья, с пестрой вышивкой на концах. Рисунок показан тут же. Рубен делается на сквозной строчке. 4¾ м полотна. 3. Практичное платье на полотна с вышитыми и настроченными полосами из белого холста. Вышивка делается прямыми стежками. Полотна—4 м, белого холста—¾ м. 4. Платье для девочки, отделанное вышивкой. Шапочка из того же материала, что и платье, отделана вышивкою того же рисунка. Рисунки худ. М. Н. Орловой.

Mariia Orlova. Sketches of womens' dresses, blouses, and childrens's frocks richly decorated with embroidery, published in the first issue of *Iskusstvo odevatsia*. 1928.

In the magazine's opening article Anatolii Lunacharsky, People's Commissar for Public Education, wrote: "There are those among us who are afraid that clothing may become elegant or coquettish, and this they consider a grave crime. It smacks, they say, of philistinism or, even worse, the bourgeoisie. In fact, a certain amount of fashion is

Блуза из кустарной ткани, вышитая тамбурным швом или крестиками. Рисунок раб. худ. М. Н. Орловой

by no means unsuited to the proletariat. . . . Of course, with each new day of our economic prosperity there will be improvements in the worker's apartment, in his food, in the way he spends his time, and, naturally, in the clothes he wears. . . ."

309
Anonymous designer. Sketches of summer dresses, costumes and bathing suits in *Iskusstvo odevatsia*. 1928.

310
L. Orshanskaia. Sketch of a coat. Ways of wearing a kerchief. Elizaveta Yakunina. Sketch of a dress. Published in *Iskusstvo odevatsia*. 1928.

85.
It was a special supplement to the review *Krasnaia panorama*.

The complex and varied aspects of creating a costume began to be tackled in earnest by the new magazine *Iskusstvo odevatsia* (The Art of Dressing) (1928),[85] the very title of which stresses the weight of the problem and its importance to the artistic community. The first issue opened with an article by Anatolii Lunacharsky, People's Commissar for Public Education, "Is This Really the Time for the Worker to be Thinking About the Art of Dressing?" The People's Commissar expressed his view of the current opinion that a fashionable costume was a "bourgeois prejudice": "There are those among us who are afraid that clothing will become elegant or coquettish, and this they consider a grave crime. It smacks, they say, of philistinism or, even worse, the bourgeoisie. Nonetheless, a certain amount of smartness and fashion is by no means unsuited to the proletariat. . . . Of course, with each new day of our economic prosperity, there will be improvements in the worker's apartment, his food, the way he spends his time, and, naturally, in the clothes he wears. . . ."[86]

86.
A. Lunacharsky, "Svoevremenno li podumat rabochemu ob iskusstve odevatsia?" in *Iskusstvo odevatsia*, 1928, no. 1, p. 3.

The same issue contained five answers to Lunacharsky's title question. The authors of the articles — workers, scientists, and artists — on the whole supported, although with some reservations, the art of dressing.

The article did not merely headline the review but also indicated the publication's general drift and the wide range of subjects to be discussed: the history of garments and textiles, the social foundations of fashion, the peculiarities of folk costume, and questions of hygiene and psychology.

Many articles were written in favor of functional, comfortable clothes. The importance of a "hygienic costume," with its own individual form, was emphasized by the People's Commissar for Public Health, N. Semashko.[87] A suitable shape and cut, he believed, was found in the Russian shirt with the collar that fastened at the side. Semashko was not alone in turning to folk costume; a number of critics upheld this point of view. Because of this, and, apparently because this opinion was shared by the editorial board of the journal, most of the models in the magazine sported folk-costume designs.

87.
Iskusstvo odevatsia, 1928, no. 3, p. 5.

Of course, the labor-consuming and complicated costume of folk traditions could not claim to be viable for industrial production — it was again addressed to the handicraft industry for one-of-a-kind manufacture. The main thrust of Soviet mass clothes was not represented here but in industrial design and broadly interpreted *prozodezhda*. Samples of *prozodezhda* did appear in *Iskusstvo odevatsia*, but only rarely. To these might be ascribed very unimpressive, poorly designed overalls for miners, and several austere suits and skirts very similar to the French styles that were so abundantly displayed in the journal.

It is worthwhile to mention several important contributors of designs. O. Anisimova published many sketches and illustrated a few covers for the magazine. Her work is distinguished by an emphatic and original interpretation of folk clothes motifs and expressive silhouettes. Anisimova was fond of a low shoulderline in a dress, sleeves that widened dramatically downwards, and short original jackets. She used Russian ornamental motifs only as a point of departure, selecting one or two elements, enlarging them, and drenching them with color so that the pattern almost resembled appliqué. Her sketches are easy to identify because of their extremely individual style. The artist was a virtuoso in interpreting folk clothes motifs in the design of contemporary costume.

309

M. Orlova created fashionable women's blouses along the same lines. Using a simple chemise-type pattern, she decorated the garment strictly in accordance with its construction, using ornament to highlight the seams or to perform the purely decorative function of color. Orlova's design shows a mastery of the laws of folk art. She is an obvious follower of Lamanova's theories, but her decoration is freer in its modernized stylization of folk motifs and color combinations. The artist could easily and convincingly incorporate in one design two separate types of decoration from different folk sources. The trimmings themselves either reproduced folk embroidery — especially Ukrainian, Russian, or Buryat — or were made of handmade fabrics or an ornamental band. She often used motifs of Kursk and Ryazan embroidery, as well as Nordic decorative motifs, while borrowing her silhouette from French fashion magazines.

310

A different trend in the journal, approaching the *prozodezhda* ideal

Пальто из шерстяной материи, вышитое гарусом.
Рисунок худ. Е. Л. Оршанской

Применение русского платка к разным фасонам платья.
Рисунок худ. Н. Л. Оршанской

Платье из материй трех синих тонов.
Рисунок худ. Якуниной

311

311

O. Anisimova. Cover of the magazine *Iskusstvo odevatsia*. 1928.

312

T. Pravosudovich, N. Orshanskaia, and M. Orlova. Sketches of costumes and sarafan dress in *Iskusstvo odevatsia*. 1928.

of the constructivists and Alexandra Exter, was represented by the artists E. Yakunina and T. Pravosudovich. Their approach was more whimsical, and also less successful. Instead of employing the constructivists' sound design principles, the artists borrowed their geometrized rhythms, though in an utterly unfounded application, and were fascinated by complex cut, nonfunctional details, and combinations of expensive and texturally different fabrics (velveteen and brocade used by Pravosudovich, or three different types of fabrics in blue tones used by Yakunina). Even in their *prozodezhda* models, where the principles of simplicity, comfort and practicality would seem bound to prevail, Yakunina concentrated on the rhythms and proportions of minor details: she supplied work clothes with many large and small pockets trimmed with decorative stitching and turned-down corners, made a right-angle notch in the lapel with buttons, and inserted two fastening tabs on the high stand-up collar. Contrasting colors — blue, yellow, orange, and green — enhanced the somewhat garish and "fashionable" effect Yakunina aspired to, even in work clothes that would be manufactured from the cheapest and plainest coarse cotton cloth.

One can see patterns of dresses and coats in *Iskusstvo odevatsia* in which vast surfaces are filled with decoration from both folk sources and constructivist designs. The designers of the ornaments included the well-known painter K. Yuon. The author of an article in the magazine, D. Aranovich, propagandizing constructivist motifs in fabrics, stressed the immense influence of "Leftist" painting, which "has pushed into the foreground . . . color, composition, texture and other formal problems. What is abstract and inexpressive as a framed painting hanging on a wall can be very impressive in fabrics, with its bias toward geometry and its response to the fondness for the machine (cogs, wheels,

Платье из креп де-шина или из какой-либо иной легкой ткани, отделано мелким
бисером или ажурной строчкой

Платье из легкой шерстяной материи, отделанное тесьмою; или же из шелка,
отделанное узкими полосками из того же материала

313

Платье из синего вельвета, отделанное окси
дированной парчей, с пестрыми полосками.
Рисунок раб. худ. Т. Правосудович

314

313

Anonymous designer. Sketches
of evening dresses in *Iskusstvo
odevatsia*. 1928.

314

T. Pravosudovich. Sketch of a
fashionable dress in *Iskusstvo
odevatsia*. 1928.

315

O. Anisimova. Sketch of a
Russian-style dress in *Iskusstvo
odevatsia*. 1928.

316

N. Orshanskaia. Sketches of
costumes; M. Orlova. Sketches of
blouses; E. Yakunina. Sketch of
an everyday dress. Published in
Iskusstvo odevatsia. 1928.

88.
D. Aranovich, "O sposobakh nanesenia risunka" in *Iskusstvo odevatsia*, 1928, no. 1, p. 11.

levers, etc.), its purely suprematist juxtaposition of color and background, bold contrast between dense adjacent colors, etc."[88]

Iskusstvo odevatsia was also the first magazine to present children's clothes, which were unsigned and, with rare exceptions, looked like copies of garments for adults. They closely resembled French designs.

The magazine lasted only two years, until 1929. Original work by Russian designers became increasingly scarce on its pages, as did articles on urgent problems of the day. In mid-1929, it began to publish more and more designs from abroad, and gradually dissociated itself from populist ideals, and consequently, its readership.

315
316

Clothing of the 1930s — Problems of an Industrial Standard

The updating of older enterprises and the construction of new ones had been launched — clothing factories appeared in Moscow, Kiev, Vitebsk, Baku, Minsk, Dnepropetrovsk, Tbilisi, and Yerevan. Special attention was paid to the creation of manufactories in the Central Asian and Transcaucasian republics, where almost none had existed in the past. Whereas in the 1920s the equipment for garment factories was imported from abroad, by the beginning of the First Five-Year Plan Soviet plants had been established, and it was hoped that they could satisfy the country's huge clothing requirements. New items included complicated machines capable of performing such processes as felling (seam stitching), pattern cutting, and sewing and tacking buttonholes. There were conveyer belts as well. Thanks to such equipment, and also to division

317

318

317

Soviet girl, member of the Komsomol and shock-worker. 1929.

318

Valentina Kulagina. *International Women Workers' Day*, poster. 1930.

The smiling girl in the photograph is a socialist emulation winner. Determined to quicken the march of history, the shock-workers, both men and women, exceeded their daily work quotas ten times. Summoned to Moscow by Stalin to discuss the targets of the First Five-Year Plan, they adopted a plan surpassing that proposed by the economists. Hundreds of thousands of young men and women in workers' overalls pinned their hopes for a better life on resolute steps, on "storm methods." They worked in the collieries of the Donets coal fields and the ore mines in Kazakhwstan, they erected the engineering works at the Urals and the Dnieper hydro-electric power station. In Kulagina's poster a multitude of exultant women are joining the Five-Year Plan workers' army. In this era of feverish industrialization, it is not the clothes, but work that makes fine men.

319

Donets coal field shock-workers.
1931.

320

Piotr Williams. *Workshop under
Construction*. 1932.

321

Firemen. 1930.

322

Alexandr Samokhvalov. *Woman
Worker*. 1928.

of labor and production line methods, by the mid-1930s labor productivity increased by 15 to 20 percent.

The task of mass producing garments in series on the factory conveyer belt made the establishment of a standard essential. What was "standard" clothing in the 1930s? There was no unified opinion, and the question raised much discussion in 1931-1932. The first to express his views on the requirement of a standard back in 1929 was the textile industry specialist, D. Smirnov, in his article "On Technology in the Garment Industry." Clothing, in his opinion, should meet climatic and hygienic requirements. In the manufacture of clothing, there must be observed "rules and norms concerning the constructive and technological component."[89] Those who feared that standardization would lead to the absolute depersonalization and a stream of identical objects were right to the extent that, with the prevailing low production levels and lack of qualified personnel, such a result was inevitable.

Almost everyone recognized the need for a standardized system of design, however, and many specialists understood that the design of functional clothing for the masses did not necessarily rule out aesthetics (what we call today the "design principles of modeling industrial series"). The standard had to be interpreted flexibly, as a basis on which to construct different types of clothing. As the critic V. Lebedev wrote: "Standard is inimical neither to the aesthetics of the future nor to the aesthetics of the transitional epoch. . . . But a standard must be dynamic, variable, and should be able to accommodate individuality."[90]

The Oktiabr (October) group, following in the footsteps of the *Lef* movement, saw

89.
D. Smirnov, "O tekhnologii v shveinoi promyshlennosti" in *Tekhnika i tekhnologia shveinoi promyshlennosti*, 1929, no. 1, pp. 4-7.

90.
V. Lebedev, "Krasivaia veshch" in *Nashi dostizhenia*, 1934, no. 6, p. 101.

322

a standard as a means to create a uniform; in their opinion, the only acceptable new type of clothing. They applied themselves to the creation of *prozodezhda*, or work clothes. The Oktiabr group hoped that professionally standardized clothing types would lead and eventually absorb all the others.

Many critics came out against this narrow, one-sided interpretation of Soviet dress, saying that a uniform was illogical. This was the opinion of E. Eikhengolts, who thought work clothes should be a separate category in which "guidance should be taken, above all, from strictly scientific data, without forgetting, however, the importance of artistic invention."[91] Function should be combined with aesthetics when mass-produced clothing is designed in any of its forms. "The task of dress designers is to find forms of clothing which, while being rational, will also be so expressive in line and colour that they produce a visual effect without the aid of applied means."[92]

But it was perhaps E. Armand who came closest to the interpretation of a standard in her article "Clothing of the Future," when she wrote that "the types of clothing devised will be as diverse as the activities of the citizens in a socialist country. . . . *Prozodezhda* alone is not enough; there must also be professional clothes, and clothes for relaxation should not be all the same. . . . Just as the ultimate aim of socialism is not total depersonalization, so, too, the objects of daily life, and above all, clothing, will not in the slightest degree lose their personality."[93]

The magazine *Shveinaia promyshlennost* (The Garment Industry), beginning in 1929, served for a decade as a monthly forum for discussion on the numerous problems of the garment

91.
E. Eikhengolts, "Problemy massovoi odezhdy" in *Sbornik: Izofront.* Moscow-Leningrad, 1931, p. 61.

92.
Ibid.

93.
E. Armand, "Odezhda budushchego" in *Shveinaia promyshlennost*, 1931, no. 12, pp. 11-12.

323

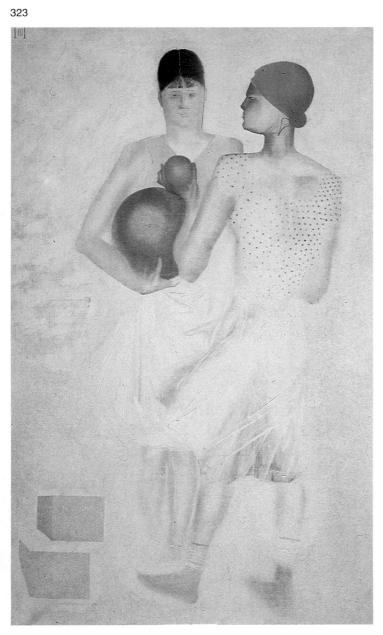

324

323
Yurii Pimenov. *Girls with a Ball.*
1929.

324
A scene from the *Blue Blouse*
performance, *The First Five-Year
Plan.* 1928.

325
Yurii Pimenov. *Spare No Effort to
Build Heavy Industry!* 1927.

325

326

326
Yurii Pimenov. *Everyone Must
Take Part in the Review!* Poster.
1928. Artists, poets, and
playwrights took to heart the
construction projects of the Five-
Year Plan. In Pimenov's paintings
and drawings, the process of
industrialization could as well be
called the "whipping up the
country" policy. Priority in
industrialization was given to
heavy industry, whereas the
construction of textile mills and
garment factories long remained
of secondary importance, which,
of course, resulted in textile and
clothing shortages.

327
Sports parade in Red Square,
Moscow. 1936. Photo by Alexandr
Rodchenko.

328
Serafima Riangina. *Rehearsal
at a Workers' Theater*. 1932.

328

330

331

329

Women's sportswear of the early 1930s.

330

Alexandr Deineka. *Physical Culture*, poster. 1933.

331

Konstantin Yuon. *Members of the Komsomol*. 1930.

In the new society, which seemed to be taking shape at the construction sites of the First Five-Year Plan, everyone was to be cheerful and strong. Hence the mass, even cultlike, enthusiasm for sports. "Work, build, and don't complain! The way to a new life is clear: you may not be an athlete but you must undergo physical training," says Deineka's poster.

industry. Although discussions centered on scientific and technological issues, they were not confined to these alone: one could find articles by leading art historians considering purely artistic problems connected with clothing design as a decorative and applied art.

The review had among its contributors specialists like M. Alpatov, E. Pribylskaia, M. Mertsalova and K. Mashurina. This magazine is almost the only source available today for studying the problems of Soviet costume in the 1930s.

Efforts were renewed during this time to train a wide range of specialists in the garment industry. Scientific organizations dealing with these problems appeared one after another throughout the decade. A research institute of the garment industry, soon reorganized into the All-Russian Scientific Research Laboratory of the Garment Industry, opened in 1930. Here methods of cutting fabric and the technical specifications of clothing manufacture were analyzed; a scientific base was being established for the production of an industrial standard. Clothing design was made an independent branch of science and assigned to special laboratories under trusts and experimental factories.

The correctly formulated tasks, however, proved impossible to accomplish. The industry, which had by that time increased the output of clothes for the masses, could not suddenly make the drastic changes required to produce high-quality standard goods.

The extremely low level of factory-manufactured garments — and obviously of industrial standards — was graphically demonstrated by the first exhibition of factory-made clothing held in 1932 at the State History Museum in Moscow. Coarse, low-quality fabrics, inept cut and slipshod execution, and, finally, the graceless features of a uniform combining the elements of a military suit and the Komsomol (Young Communist League) clothes of the 1920s, made the new clothing unattractive and shapeless. Most of the designs showed a complete ignorance of artistic and constructional principles. The lack of awareness of the fabrics' properties led to cotton dresses that were designed as silk, and to elegant garments that combined heavy, textured wool with thin and light materials. As before, the functions of professional artists at the factories

332

Physical culture parade in
Moscow's Red Square. 1936.
Photo by Alexandr Rodchenko.

333

Vladimir Lebedev. *A Girl in a
Football Jersey with a Bunch
of Flowers*. 1933.

334

A group of young people in
bathing suits by the sea. Early
1930s. The cult of athletics
transformed sport. While in the
1920s these clothes were central
to formal searches of the
constructivist designers, in the
1930s, when physical strength was
exalted, they served convenience
alone. The artificiality of fashion
disappeared. Clothes became the
second skin for strong bodies
ready for work and for defense
of the country.

332

333

334

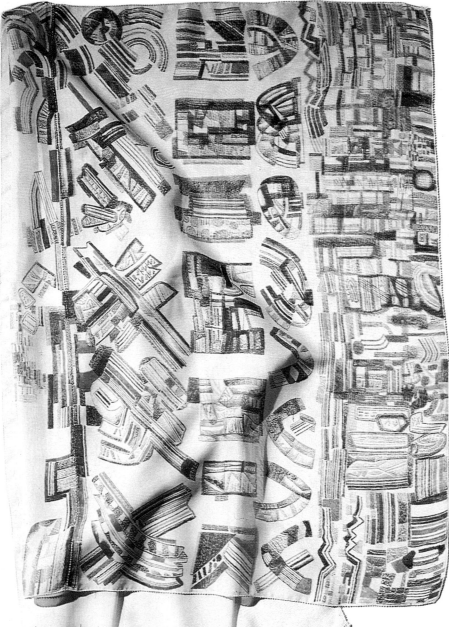

335

336

335

Pavel Filonov. *Scarf*. 1930s.

336

Zolotareva. Cotton print. Early
1930s.

337

Anonymous designer. Cotton print.
1930.

338, 339

F. Antonov. Cotton prints. Early
1930s.

340

Alexandr Samokhvalov. *Weaving
Workshop*. 1934.

341

F. Antonov. *Modern Rhythms*,
cotton print. Early 1930s.

342

Anonymous designer. *Sailor*,
cotton print. Early 1930s.

337
338
339

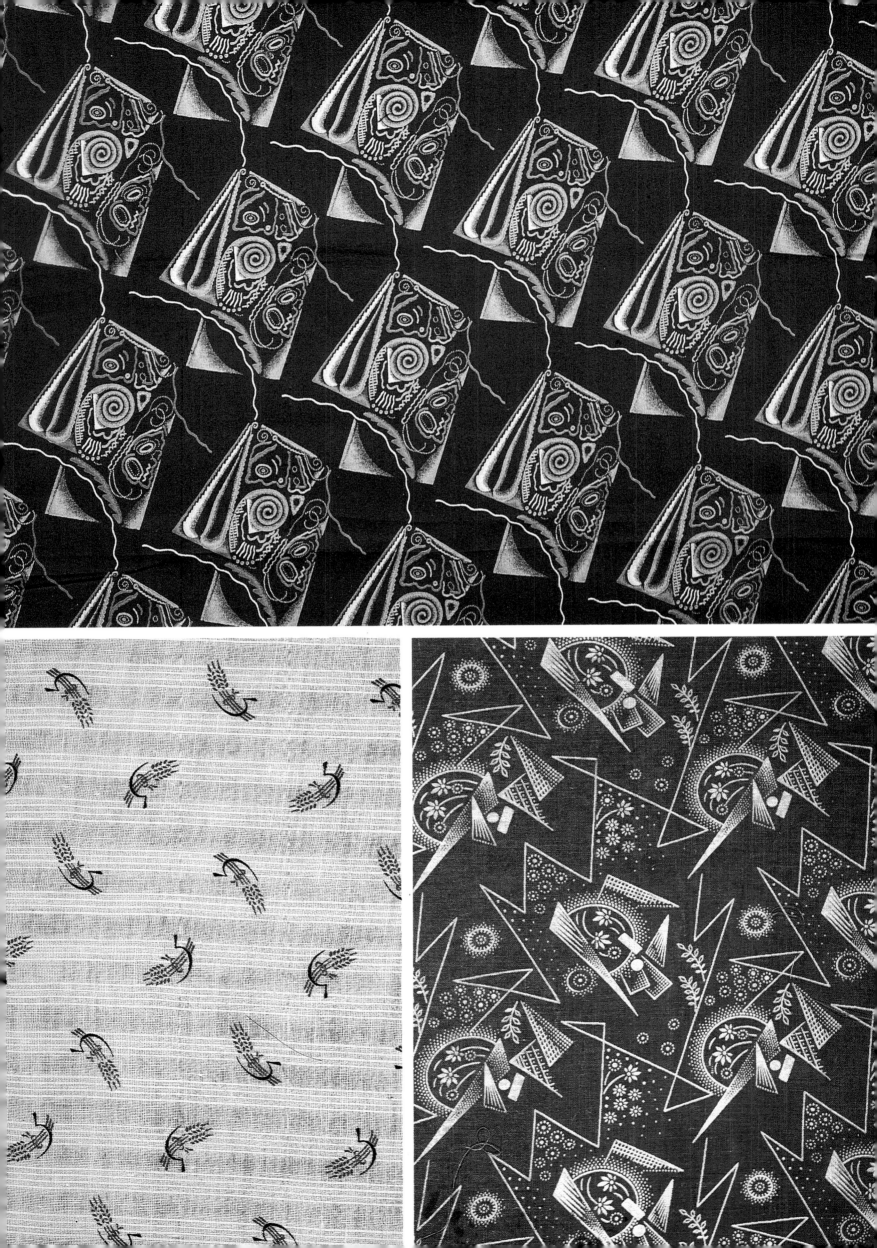

were not infrequently performed by the old "hack" designers who understood nothing of the creative challenges of modern costume and often settled for blandly copying (usually badly) fashion plates from foreign publications. They believed that any item could be made fashionable simply by adding stylish details.

Only slightly better were specialized work clothes for varied professions. They at least indicated a desire to proceed from a logical cut and the specificity and diversity of professional functions. This section exhibited sailors' waterproofs, fishermen's suits, special clothes for workers in boiler rooms, and clothes for chemical plant personnel. Accessories for *prozodezhda* were also on display: boots, crash helmets, overalls, and gauntlets made of special fabrics. Nevertheless, from the point of view of industrial design, these models were feeble and inefficient.

This was also true of clothes for the collective-farm village. Models of women's dresses repeated the traditional forms of a full calico skirt and a blouse with a basque fitted at the waist. In the 1930s these farm villages were supplied, in fact, with the same kind of mass-produced goods as in pre-revolutionary times. Instead of short coats suitable for farm work and practical overalls and trousers made of light fabrics,

340
341
342
343

343

A fancy needlework circle. 1930s. In the 1930s the textile industry was still in crisis. Restoring and operating prerevolutionary enterprises was the only possible solution. They were amalgamated into one trust, and the work of the designing departments at the factories was regulated. This is why tractors and grain harvesters disappeared from calicos so quickly after the governmental decision on "inappropriate designs," with only stylized motifs remaining. In spite of so much effort, however, textile shortages remained. This is why amateur dressmaking and needlework circles were so popular at the workers' clubs and cultural centers.

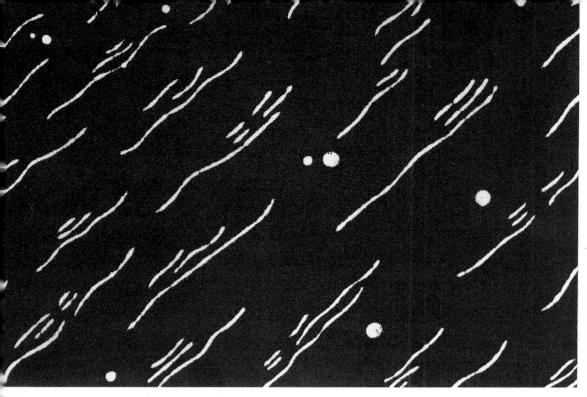

344

Anonymous designer. *Milky Way*,
silk design. 1933.

345

Anonymous designer. *Starry Sky*,
silk design. Mid-1930s.

346, 347

Anonymous designer. Silk fabrics
with a plant motif. 1932-1934.
Silk fabrics remained almost
untouched by the infatuation with
thematic designs. Proponents of
textiles' propaganda role
repeatedly attacked their
Shelkotrest (Silk Trust) colleagues
for avoiding "daring innovations."
These elegant textiles with
astronomic and plant motifs were
more than once derided in the
press of those years as "pitiable,
monotonous, and dull-colored."

people received heavy and cumbersome men's thick wool overcoats, and expensive men's suits and women's coats.

Of all the types of everyday wear, only clothes for the collective farm remained untouched. Only its broadest principles had been formulated. In 1930, Mashurina published in *Shveinaia promyshlennost* an article "On the Problem of Forms of Clothes for the Industrial Countryside," which discussed designing special series of clothes for the collective farmers: "With the growth and complication of production, the country-side has mechanically adopted urban clothes. The present-day "peasant" clothes are cheaper substitutes of urban articles. The new form of rural economy — the collective-farm system — dictates new forms of clothing as well. The problem of the peasant costume is to be seen not in "folk patterns" but in the requirements of work and the workers' physical environment."[94] Mashurina stressed that the design of standard clothes for collective farmers must be based on the laws of correspondence between form, fabric, and purpose: Lamanova's formula. Garment factories, however, consistently disregarded these requirements.

The absence of skilled clothing designers who could create standard models for quantity production resulted in the industry mastering the manufacture of only a few primitive types of light and outer clothes evidently "designed" in the factory workshops. This gave occasion to art critics and writers to attack this type of clothing in a number of articles. The most strident and irrefutable of them was "The Decreed Bow" by Ilia Ilf and Evgenii Petro. "The whole of the Soviet Union is supplied with two clumsy types of coats, three dull types of men's suits, and four appalling kind's of women's dresses. These are all that are manufactured, and there is no escaping them. All men and women are compelled to dress according to this single style."[95] The very title of the article mocks designers who lack a "flight of intellect" and creativity, and who await instructions from their superiors on how and what to make.

The everyday or street fashion that was not produced industrially differed little from that of the previous decade, and continued spontaneously to include simple, comfortable and, what was most important, inexpensive articles: blouses and long skirts, striped shorts, jerseys, knitted

94.
K. Mashirina, "K probleme form odezhdy industrialnoi derevni" in *Shveinaia promyshlennost*, 1930, no. 910, pp. 35-36.

95.
I. Ilf and E. Petrov, "Direktivnyi bantik" in the book *Felietony*. Moscow, 1965, p. 6.

berets and kerchiefs, wide linen trousers, and occasionally military-style riding-breeches and lightweight skirts of simple cut. They constituted, indeed, the "mass series," often made by the home sewer. The tendency toward lightness, comfort and sportiness was in line with the enthusiasm for physical culture, which in the 1930s became truly universal.

The garment industry's noticeable lag behind other branches of production and the low quality of clothes and footwear made the highest Party committees adopt, in 1931-1933, several special decisions concerning the quality and range of mass-produced articles and the level of their standard. They recognized the need to radically improve ready-made clothes and to combat the output of poor, crudely tailored, and tastelessly designed garments.

Lasting benefits resulted from the years of discussion on the "textile language," its possibilities, limitations and relationship with the costume. An end was eventually put to designers' hackneyed approach to their work. The art studios that sprang up in textile factories began to include in their curricula trips to different parts of the country, sketching from nature, and research in museum collections of folk art. In 1933 more attention began to be given to designs based on natural motifs. Flowers, leaves, sprigs, and stalks of rye, subtly but clearly drawn, were freely distributed on a plain ground. In light fabrics like voile or marquisette, a small, simple design was used to emphasize the soft and airy texture of the fabric. Designers based textile motifs on their drawings from nature, reworked, however, to suit their transformation into dress fabrics. Textile designers included well-known names such as M. Khvostenko, V. Skliarova, S. Agaian, N. Shukhaev, N. Kirsanova, and many others.

As in the 1920s, the problems of mass-produced clothes and of improvements in light industry in the 1930s were dealt with in the context of raising the culture of production as a whole and of combatting "philistinism." In architecture, too, questions were raised on form and function. Discussions began on the development of fundamentals for designing residential houses, with some critics seeing a house as a featureless "machine for dwelling," a product of engineering that performed merely utilitarian functions; while others took into account the

348, 349

V. Gurkovskaia. Cotton prints with a plant design. Mid-1930s.

350

Fashionable dress of the mid-1930s. Plant designs, branded by the constructivists and advocates of thematic design as ''bourgeois'' and ''vulgar,'' gradually shook off these labels. As a matter of fact, the manufacture of floral calicos for the countryside and for export never ceased, and quantitatively even prevailed over all the current trends. By the mid-1930s, plant motifs became extremely popular. Townswomen made dresses of floral-patterned fabrics with lightly fitted waists and flared skirts that showed their figures to advantage.

348
349
350

354

355

351

352

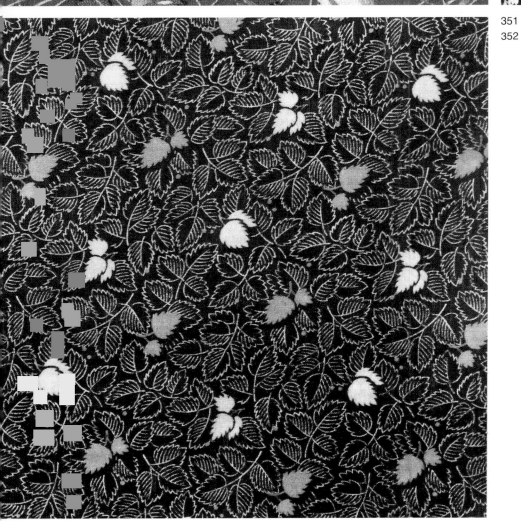

353

96.
M. Alpatov, "Kakoi kostium nam nuzhen?" in *Brigada khudozhnikov*, no. 6, 1932, p. 51.

dual nature of architecture — function and beauty. This was the approach of the well-known art historian M. Alpatov; in architecture and the decorative and applied arts, he stressed aesthetics. He wrote of the necessity to regard creative activity from two points of view, "not only as utilitarian but also as having an artistic and ideological function, just as we see in architecture not only a 'dwelling machine' but also a form of art."[96]

In the first half of the 1930s, the technical and economic growth of the textile industry accelerated somewhat, and this made the need for decisive action even more urgent. The complex aesthetic problems of clothing, particularly concerning its placement in the category of works of decorative and applied arts, had to be reappraised. This concept was not new: the idea of mass clothing as a distinct sphere of art had long been discussed, and definite progress had been made by the pioneers of Soviet costume in the previous decade. It was now necessary to establish an efficient center of dress design that would develop the principles and supply the samples for standards of mass production.

356

357

Creation of the Moscow House of Clothing Design — Designers of the 1930s

97.
Shveinaia promyshlennost, no. 5, 1933, p. 65; no. 1, 1933, p. 23; no. 6, 1933, pp. 1-2; no. 10, 1934, pp. 11-13.

Ideas concerning "institutes of clothing" or "design houses" had been circulating since the early 1930s, and were repeatedly mentioned in the fashion press.[97] Some of the functions of these houses, though on a rather small scale, were performed by the laboratories maintained by trusts. One of them, the Moskvoshvei (Moscow Garment) experimental laboratory, became the foundation on which the Moscow House of Clothing Design was built in 1934. Already at the time of its creation, its main task was declared to be teamwork between artists and designers, for only such work made it possible to foresee all the nuances of combined technical and artistic problem-solving in preparing clothes for serial production. This formed the backbone of the creative activities of the artists of the Moscow House of Clothing Design. Its functions also included control over the performance of garment factories and the study of their potential for producing series of mass-consumption goods.

The first director of this house was Lamanova's student and follower Nadezhda Makarova (1898-1969). She invited a nucleus of gifted artists to work with her, among them F. Gorelenkova, also Lamanova's student, A. Liamina, E. Raizman, and some talented artists of theater costume: S. Taplianinov and A. Sudakevich, as well as dress designers. Most of them did not have special training; they were gifted self-taught artists with a rich experience of practical work.

An important part was played by the Art Council at the House of

358

356, 357
B. Iofan, V. Shchuko, V. Gelfreikh. Competition design and model of the Palace of Soviets. 1932-1933.

358
A Woman shock-worker. 1933. The first workers' and peasants' state was aware of its historical and cultural uniqueness, and tried to immortalize its as yet unrivaled magnificence. The Palace of Soviets, a grandiose edifice crowned with a 100-meter-high statue of Lenin that would reach the clouds, ossified at the design stage. This unfinished project ironically reflected the emerging hierachy of the new society. The builders found themselves at the very bottom of the pyramid. In the new world of fraternity no distinctions were to be made between town and country, or between intellectual and manual labor.

Clothing Design, which included, along with designers, prominent personalities in the art world like V. Favorsky, V. Mukhina, A. Goncharov, D. Arkin, and Y. Pimenov.

As Makarova recalled: "Council meetings turned into real artistic discussions, in which each item was debated from every angle. Such encounters were extremely helpful in putting dress designers on the right track."[98]

It was in those years that artists began to work systematically on sketches for future designs, aware that this was an essential part of the creative process. By jotting down ideas on paper, the artist focused on the integrity of the artistic treatment, developing his own stamp and style of presentation. Gradually this graphic expression of clothing design became an independent genre, acquiring by the 1960s a special niche in the fashion art world.

98.
Nadezhda Makarova's notes.
Manuscript.

359
360
361
362

359
Shock-workers of the Kramatorsk Metallurgical Plant. 1931.

360
Gustav Klutsis. *Young Komsomol Members, Be Among the Best in the Sowing Campaign!* Poster. 1931.

361
Gustav Klutsis. *Long Live the USSR, the Homeland for the Working People throughout the World!* Poster. 1931.

362
Construction of a public building in Moscow. Early 1930s. During the First Five-Year Plan, Soviet Russia became one huge construction site: "The Homeland for the Working People throughout the World" contrasted starkly with the bourgeois world experiencing its worst depression. Klutsis created in his photomontage posters a world of mammoth dimensions, a future world populated with the shock-workers of today. These titans, as portrayed in the magazines and newspapers, were the Donets coal-field miners, Kramatorsk metallurgists, builders of the Moscow subway and the majestic public buildings with which Moscow, capital of the world proletariat, began to be embellished.

363
Kazimir Malevich. *Woman Worker*.
1933.

364

Kazimir Malevich. *Portrait of the
Artist's Wife*. 1933.

365-367

Mikhail Bobyshov. Sketches of costumes for the play *The Bright Stream*. 1935. Water worship seized the USSR, and canals were built all over the country. Water was to decorate the state's capital, and Moscow's embankments were to be its most beautiful streets. Waves became popular fabric motifs.

367

From the very beginning of the 1930s, women's fashion design in Europe was taken over by a new set of principles: the straight silhouette was replaced by a close-fitting one that emphasized the shape of the body. With this came a change in the whole system of dress construction and decoration. Longer dresses with a perforated waist became fashionable, trimmed with decorative stitching, flounces, and ornamental buttons.

In Soviet Russia, however, the new trends arrived in the second half of the 1930s, leaving their imprint first on fashion magazines. Until then, the Moscow House of Clothing Design still applied Lamanova's principles of comfortable and functional clothing of simple construction, which were so important in mass production. Until the late 1920s, this trend was supported by Makarova. At the turn of the decade, however, Makarova's individual style became more pronounced. She designed quite a few samples of various types of everyday clothes that were easy to manufacture in serial production. At the same time she continued her favorite work on garments in which she used folk costume motifs. But if in the previous decade her designs showed a tendency to incorporate motifs from Russian folk costume, in the 1930s she drew most often on the national dress of peoples of the North, the Ukraine, and Transcaucasia. At the international fur trader exhibition in Leipzig (1930), Makarova exhibited a ski suit whose cut and decoration were those of Nenets clothes. There were caps and winter jackets trimmed with long-piled fur at the cuffs and pockets, and bright orange stripes inspired by Nenets design. The combination of soft beige fabric with brown fluffy fur and bright-colored trim was extremely effective. Makarova was one of the first to design charming and bright garments for children, embellishing them with patterned folk ornaments.

The first group of artists employed at the Moscow House of Clothing Design — F. Gorelenkova, A. Liamina, S. Toplianinov, and V. Danilina — displayed the same tendency toward simplicity as their director. Gorelenkova, who started her career in Lamanova's studio, was chiefly interested in the expressiveness of a garment's shape. She had a subtle feeling for its "sculpturesque" quality, and stressed its harmony of

368

Efim Cheptsov. *School Teachers*. 1925. The government announced that general education was an outcome of the October Revolution. "Formerly a privilege of the few, education has become accessible to all" — these words were cut in stone on monuments to the fallen fighters of the revolution. The way to socialism lay not only through industrialization and cooperation of agriculture but also through the education of the people: in political jargon this was called "the third front." Here we see teachers gathered for a meeting in a crowded village schoolroom. The men wear soldier's blouses and Tolstoy-style shirts, the Russian intellectuals' uniform in the late 19th century, and women wear dresses and blouses of homespun linen. The magazines *Rabocheie prosveshchenie* (Workers' Education) and *Tretii front* (The Third Front) are piled on the table.

construction. The artist obviously tried to take into account how her dresses would look on the wearer, both in one-of-a-kind garments and in factory designs to be produced in quantity.

A popular idea in the 1930s was to make everyday clothing for men and women more like sports clothes. Toplianinov, who had come to the House of Clothing Design from the Bolshoi Theater costume workshops, consistently carried this idea into effect: instead of traditional coats he designed sports jackets of a soft silhouette, without a lining or lapels. Buttons were replaced with snaps or zippers. He also designed women's "dress-pants," as overalls were then called, and though they looked rather unprepossessing they were convenient for work and sports. Toplianinov's efforts toward useful everyday clothes found supporters among the critics; one of them was V. Shekhman, a regular contributor to the review *Shveinaia promyshlennost*.[99]

In 1934-1935, eight dressmaking and tailoring establishments were opened under the House of Clothing Design. Garments designed in these establishments could be offered to clients only after approval by the Art Council of the House of Clothing Design. The advantage of this system

99.
Shveinaia promyshlennost, no. 5, 1933, p. 65; no. 1, 1933, p. 23; no. 6, 1933, pp.1-2; no. 10, 1934, pp. 11-13.

368
369
370

369
Konstantin Youn. *High School Students*. 1929.

370
Konstantin Istomin. *Students*. 1933. The battle of socialism was being won on the cultural revolution front. Hundreds of thousands of boys and girls, carefully selected by committees that did not examine their level of knowledge (there were no entrance examinations up to the mid-1930s) but their proletarian origin, came to the famed universities of Russia. The clothes of the Moscow university students testify to their "good record": the women workers' kerchiefs, the workers' Russian shirts, peaked and cloth caps, and the Red Army soldiers' uniform.

371

Natalia Kiseleva (1906-1951)

Natalia Fedorovna Kiseleva was born in a peasant family in Samara in 1906. After moving to Moscow in 1923, she entered the Profintern School Teachers' Training College, from which she graduated in 1927. Then Kiseleva decided to enter the Higher State Technical Art Studios and chose the profession of textile designer. In those years instructors there included such remarkable artists as N. Udaltsova, L. Maiakovskaia, and N. Kupreianov. Kiseleva's creative principles also developed under the impact of A. Rodchenko, V. Stepanova, and L. Popova. In 1930, the artist joined the art department of the Moscow Textile Institute, from which she graduated in 1931.

During her school years, Kiseleva created a large number of textile ornaments in a spirit of painterly cubism, revealing an unmistakable gift as a decorative colorist. Stylistically the artist's work is close to both the constructivists' painting and the textile design of L. Maiakovskaia.

After the completion of her studies, Kiseleva was hired at the Moscow Garment Factory, where she started her career as a designer of *prozodezhda* and sports clothes. At the same time she made textile designs for the Red Rose Integrated Factories.

From the mid-1930s on, Kiseleva worked for theaters (the Stalingrad Regional Theater) and designed costumes for physical culture parades in Moscow (commissioned by the textile workers' sports society, Plamia). On the eve of the war and afterwards, Kiseleva worked for the Military Literature Publishers, where she designed training posters for the Red Army.

371

Natalia Kiseleva. Fabric design. Late 1920s.

372

Natalia Kiseleva as a student. 1927.

373, 374

Natalia Kiseleva. Fabric design. Late 1920s. At the very height of the enthusiasm for thematic textile designs, the young artist Natalia Kiseleva remained faithful to her VKhUTEMAS teachers and her idols, the constructivists. When the textile mills were producing calicos sporting airplanes and tractors, she created geometric designs, not only of her tutors' predilection but also of her own individual style.

was that it helped to raise general awareness of good clothing design.

In 1936, a special department for training clothing artists and designers was set up at the Moscow Textile Institute on the initiative of Fedorov-Davydov, the artist and instructor P. Pashkov, and the artist Liamina. A factory and an atelier of children's clothes also opened in the capital. For the first time professional artists were designing clothes specifically for children, instead of the usual miniature copies of adult garments.

The children's clothes designer V. Shterenberg, like Bozhneva and Vysheslavtseva soon after him, designed clothes for children of different age groups in which ornamentation, inventiveness and comfort predominated. Bozhneva's and Vysheslavtseva's careers started at the knitwear factory in Kosino, near Moscow. What particularly interested these artists was simultaneously designing the fabric and the clothes, and they developed a new technique for producing knit fabrics interwoven with colored stripes. By combining the stripes and sometimes adding

375, 376

Natalia Kiseleva. Fabric designs. Late 1920s — early 1930s. Kiseleva was a master of textile design techniques. The geometric blue-and-green pattern might have been created in 1934, when Kiseleva was learning Maiakovskaia's spray-painting technique.

377

Piotr Konchalovsky. *Portrait of the Actress Angelina Stepanova*. 1933.

378

Natalia Kiseleva. *Portrait of the Artist's Sister*. 1936. While working as a designer at one of the Moscow garment factories in the 1930s, Kiseleva devoted her leisure time to drawing and painting: she created fabric designs and painted portraits of her relatives. She represented her sister, a historian, in a fashionable skirt and bolero jacket. An accentuated waistline and feminine silhouette were the characteristic features of the 1930s costume.

375

376

a pattern, they created a foundation for designs inspired by folk motifs. The artists went on expeditions throughout the country, worked a great deal in museums, and studied design. Like many of their predecessors, these artists continually preferred the creative interpretation of folk clothes to the unwavering use of traditional folk motifs. Their approach was more natural and, what was most important, more promising: it was the approach used by Western fashion — free invention within the framework of industrial design.

Bozhneva and Vysheslavtseva designed several series of women's and children's dresses, blouses, and coats in knitted fabrics.

They were generally distinguished by highly professional construction, decorativeness and elegance, and a skillful use of typically Russian designs.

They created children's clothes in ensembles of long pants, jackets,

379

379, 380
Natalia Kiseleva. Fabric designs.
Late 1920s.

381
Natalia Kiseleva. Design for a
tablecloth. Late 1920s.
These are the artist's student
works. After her constructivist
period influenced by Stepanova
and Rodchenko, she created
compositions in the spirit of
Kandinsky.

380

381

382

384

383

385

and caps. Some included simplified modifications of decoration used by the peoples of Northern Russia, others by the inhabitants of Central Russia. Their designs often contrasted smooth panels of knitted wool with alternating vertical or horizontal colored stripes, emphasizing the constructive elements of the garment. Here, too, use was made of the fundamentals of folk-style cut, especially in the shoulderline and the piping on the sleeves. The shoulder seams were shifted to the back and bodice and were edged with decorative piping. Stylistically, too, these designs followed Lamanova's, with a round-necked chemise-cut blouse, sometimes with a belt that was flat or woven into the form of a cord. The soft knitted fabric shaped the body, while its bright hues gave it a folk-style holiday look.

The designers' children's ensembles existed both in single samples and in industrially produced series. They sometimes used in woollen knitted fabrics motifs of fur patterns, which in a different material and with machine manufacture acquired greater geometry, organization, and precision. A knitted children's dress might include, for example, a "knitted" form of a sarafan, and Kursk folk ornament motifs combined with smooth and patterned stripes. The Kosino knitwear factory managed to produce

382, 384, 385
Natalia Kiseleva. Sketches of sports clothes. Early 1930s.

383
Alexandr Keineka. Sketch of a costume for a theater performance. Early 1930s.

386
Nina Aizenberg. Sketch of a sport costume for an amateur performance. 1927-1931.

387
Natalia Kiseleva. Sketch of a woman's costume. Early 1930s.

388
F. Antonov. *Football*, wallpaper design. Early 1930s.
Like most of the VKhUᵀEMAS students, Kiseleva was keen on sports. She liked designing sports clothes and was especially good at men's suits.

389

Сотрудница интуриста

берет - фетровый

пальто
из рогожки
швы выстрочены
перьсом толстым
шелком

пуговицы - кожаные
пряжки на поясе и рук.
кожаные
шарф газ.

кожи-де-шина
п рафарленной

перчатки из
натуральной
замши пом.
белые

т. А Крименцу
85

389
Ignatii Nivinsky. Sketch of a costume for I. Mikitenko's play *A Matter of Honor*. 1931.

390
Natalia Kiseleva. Sketches of women's dresses. Mid-1930s.

391
A coat and a beret, as popular in the 1930s as the red kerchief was in the 1920s.

392-395
Natalia Kiseleva. Sketches of men's and women's sports uniforms, a woman's dress and coat. Mid-1930s. In the 1930s the militarization of Soviet society was reflected in clothes: the ideal citizen was broad-shouldered and had a soldierly haircut, ready both for work and the defense of Soviet Russia.

391

390

this technologically intricate model in some quantity. One-third of all the knitted garments produced in those years were made of cotton; unfortunately they were usually sweaters of simple construction and jackets of the same plain shape, dull color and low quality.

A highly original designer in the 1930s was Natalia Kiseleva, a gifted artist who, nevertheless, has remained relatively unknown.[100] She was one of the few textile artists who received professional education in the 1920s. From 1927 to 1930 she studied at the textile department of the Higher State Technical Art Studios, and then entered the textile design department of the Moscow Textile Institute, where her instructors were A. Goncharova, N. Udaltsova, and S. Gerasimov. At the Red Rose Silk Combine, where Kiseleva was hired in 1931, she made the acquaintance of Maiakovskaia, who had a great influence on her. She also worked side by side with the constructivists Stepanova and Rodchenko.

Kiseleva began to design textiles in the late 1920s. The tide of constructivist experiments had subsided, but not without leaving a strong impression in its wake. Kiseleva's designs were usually complicated in form, structure and coloring. One of the simplest is a little geometric pattern of black triangles in which the ground consists of the same shapes but larger, in a subdued grey tone. The pattern has a second "layer" made up of parts of a circle in shaded turquoise, and gives an impression of outward simplicity and a fine, ingrained complexity, as many-layered as Stepanova's later works. Kiseleva's ornate designs often

100.
See T. Strizhenova, "N. Kiseleva" in *Zhurnal mod*, 1987.

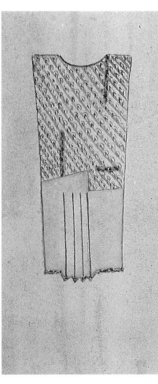

396

396, 397, 399, 400, 401
N. Anzimirova. Sketches of sports suits for a *Blue Blouse* performance. 1930.

398
Alexandr Deineka. *Collective Farmer! Keep Up Physical Exercise!* Poster. 1930.

397

401

399
400

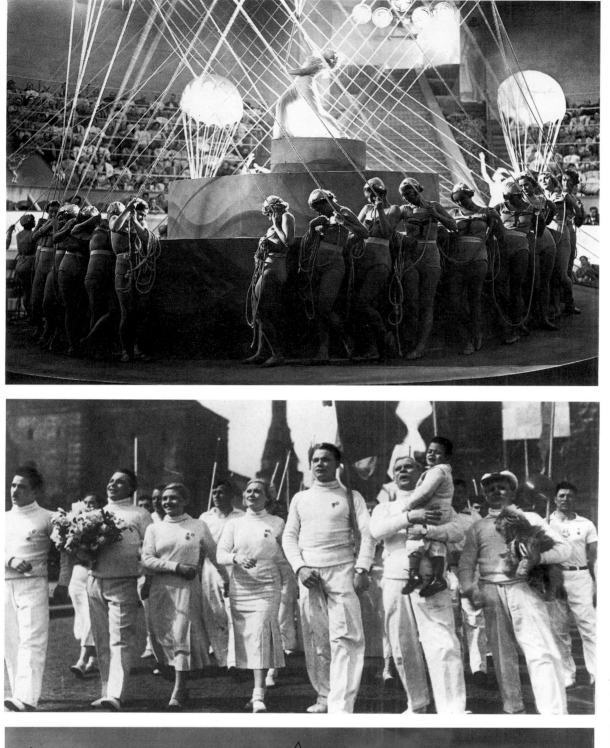

402-404

Frames from G. Alexandrov's film
The Circus. 1936.

405

Piotr Williams. *Woman Acrobat*.
1927.

406, 407

N. Anzimirova. Sketches of sports
suits for a *Blue Blouse*
performance. 1930.
Sports festivals, physical culture
parades, processions, and
meetings reached an
unprecedented scale in the 1930s.
Participation in these collective
rituals was obligatory.

402
403
404   405

included crossing lines, superimposed shapes, and geometric lines combined with painterly color patches. Her sketches also give an impression of painterly softness, not so much by the motif as by the shading of the surface, where rich hues gradually fade into half-tones. Kiseleva used a special technique she learned under the guidance of Maiakovskaia: she spray-painted with an airbrush, making the surface of the fabric shimmer. While in her fabrics of the late 1920s Kiseleva followed the constructivist style, from the early 1930s, when she worked for the Red Rose Combine, she executed many sketches in a spirit of *agittema*. One can see here airplane motifs and thematic emblems and motifs, as in, for example, "Cotton Picking".

Since the late 1920s, when she began to design at the Moskvoshvei garment factory, Kiseleva revealed an interesting idiosyncrasy: she almost never used her textile designs in her garment designs — for her these were two independent and unconnected sectors of activity. Perhaps she did not see her fabrics as a "semi-finished product;" her fabric designs on paper were more like drawings in their own right. This was not unlike Alexandra Exter's attitude toward painting: her painterly motifs were never used in her clothing designs.

406

408

409

408
Ilia Mashkov. *Young Pioneer with a Bugle*. 1933.

409
Fiodor Bogorodsky. *A Red Sailor*. 1932.

410
N. Anzimirova. Sketch of a Red Army uniform for a *Blue Blouse* performance, *Our Cavalry*. 1930.

411
Fiodor Bogorodsky. *At the Photographer's*. 1932.
Few changes were made in seamen's clothes after the revolution, unlike the Red Army uniform, which was being redesigned by accomplished artists on the instructions of the Bolshevik government. The sailor's suit was a consistently popular item in everyday life. Before the 1917 Revolution it was worn by boys in aristocratic families, and in the years of Soviet power it was adopted by the Young Pioneers, the young guard of the Communist Party.

Sketches of everyday dresses by Kiseleva often show the geometrization of construction typical of the *Lef* group. The design for a mini dress (the only one with a simple printed pattern) displays a geometric scheme and meticulous attention to its distribution, to the dress's decorative elements, and even to the number of pleats on the skirt. She addressed these designs to her contemporaries, describing in detail on her sketch how the finished dress should look.

Natalia Kiseleva created fashionable ensembles as well. Their French origin is obvious — the artist kept an eye on the fashion of her time, reinterpreting it in her own style. Typical of a French-influenced design, for instance, was the ensemble modelled by her sister: a blouse with sleeves widened toward the end, a short jacket, and a narrow, straight skirt.

The field Natalia Kiseleva most enjoyed was sports clothes, which she designed throughout the 1930s. She herself was an avid oarsman. Photographs portray the artist as slender and athletic-looking. She designed sports clothes as though they were for herself, with functionality, comfort, simplicity, and freedom from unnecessary details, but regarded elegance and beauty as absolutely essential. Like the Lef group, Kiseleva rejected all but color ornamentation in sport clothes.

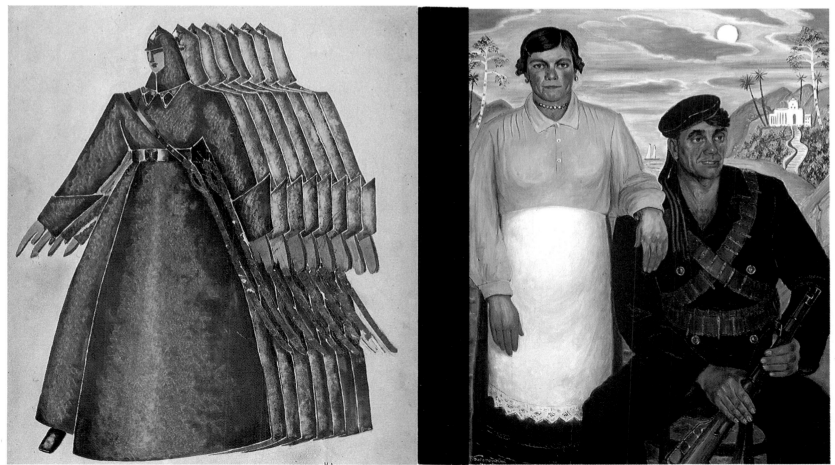

412

413

412

Piotr Shukhmin. *Militiaman at His Post*. 1932.

413

N. Anzimirova. Sketch of a costume for a *Blue Blouse* performance. 1931.

414

Nikolai Dormidontov. *Skier*. 1931.

415

Alexandr Samokhvalov. *Member of Osoaviakhim*, sketch of the painting *Militarized Komsomol*. 1932.

416

Konstantin Vialov. *The Kronstadt Roadstead*. 1928. A man in military clothes or uniform was a fashion icon in the 1930s and therefore an example to be followed. Fashion applied not only to clothes but also to faces, attitudes and gestures.

417

417

Georgii Bibikov. *Osoaviakhim Dirigible*. 1935.

418

Ekaterina Zernova. *Handing Over the Tanks*. 1931.

419

Mariia Bri-Bein. *Radio Operators*. 1930.

Military equipment pervaded everyday life. Many people were members of the voluntary Society fo the Promotion of Defense, Aviation, and Chemical Industry (Osoaviakhim). This society's membership dues were used for the military training of schoolboys and high school students, and to supply barrage balloons and other equipment. In illustration 417 Bibikov shows the lauching of a balloon. Factory workers and employees surrendered part of their already scanty wages to make military hardware for the army. Zernova depicted the thrilling moment of unity between the army and the people. The tanks were built with money donated by the workers of the textile and metallurgical industry.

Her shirts for a woman athlete and a football player are extremely simple and light. In the tourist outfit, as well, everything is well planned: the small peaked cap covers the ears; the long tight-fitting jacket has a yoke and large pockets. The cap and the jacket are grey and brown. The long comfortable mittens and the scarf are red and white, and the ensemble includes thick-soled shoes. A very practical construction and elegant proportions (wide shoulders and a narrow waist and hips), plus refined color combinations, make this model timeless and classic. Her sketches contain quite a few ski suits, showing the figure in motion to demonstrate how the suit will move with the body. Kiseleva also enjoyed designing suit jackets. She especially liked lightweight suits with short trousers, overalls with convenient, attractive patch pockets, and unusual closures. Her suit designs were simple, matter-of-fact and highly professional, though lacking any of the marks of individuality that distinguished Alexandra Exter's contemporaneous work. In 1938-1939 Kiseleva made decorations for physical culture parades in Moscow on behalf of the textile workers' sports society, Plamia.

Like many other clothes designers of her era, Keseleva also made theater costumes and stage sets, when she worked for the Stalingrad

419

420

423

424

420, 423
Ignatii Nivinsky. Sketch of men's suits for V. Kirshon's play *The Trial*. 1933.

421
Nina Aizenberg. Sketch of a costume for the play *To Be Regretted*. 1937.

422
Frame from G. Alexandrov's film *Merry Fellows*. 1934.

424
Yulii Ganf. Caricature from the satirical review *Krokodil* (Crocodile) of 1929. The clothes of mid-1930s Soviet workers and intellectuals generally resembled those of Europeans. This is evident when comparing Nivinsky's theater sketches, Aizemberg's sketches, a frame from the very popular film *Merry Fellows*, and Ganf's caricature. The latter portrays an office clerk and a worker, and is supplied with a sinister inscription: "A puzzle for little Party children: which of the two is cleaner? Answers to be sent to the nearest control committee."

regional theater. Much can be learned about the nature of clothes in the 1930s from the theater artists' work for contemporary authors' plays. Their sketches reveal which fabrics or dress details were popular, how people wore garments and moved in them. A wide range of characters from different social groups and their respective garments are depicted in the sketches of I. Nivinsky, who designed costumes for the play *A Matter of Honor*.

Because of the systematic attempts to create clothes for the masses, critics began showing a deeper interest in the purely artistic aspects of the problems involved: the history of costume of different countries and peoples, the evolution of form, and the role of the silhouette, line and construction, decorative elements, color, and composition.[101]

Articles in the press began concretely analyzing this complex phenomenon, fashion. A number of art historians (including E. Eikhengolts and M. Mertsalova) asserted that it was reckless for Soviet dress design to diverge radically from Western fashion. ''We are now living

101.
In 1936 the review *Shveinaia promyshlennost* began regularly publishing articles on European fashions.

425, 426

Valentina Khodasevich. Sketches of costumes for A. Faiko's play *A Thankless Role*. 1932.

427

Nina Aizenberg. Sketch of a costume for A. Korneichuk's play *Platon Krechet*. 1936.

428

Nina Aizenberg. Sketch of a costume for the play *People in White Smocks*. 1934.

429

Alexandr Deineka. Sketch of a costume for V. Maiakovsky's play *Bath*. 1930. The frequently criticized but most powerful stratum of Soviet society, the bureaucracy, began to create its own style in the 1930s. As they changed in accordance with fashion, the clothes of the Soviet official became instantly recognizable, and the men's suit and tie, long treated as "bourgeois," were vindicated.

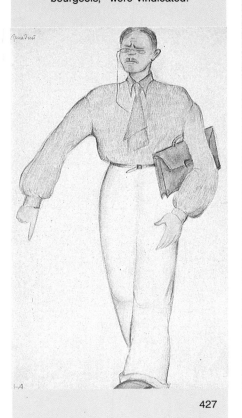

427

428

429

430

432

431   433

430, 432, 435, 437
Ignatii Nivinsky. Sketches of
costumes for I. Mikitenko's play
A Matter of Honor. 1931.

431, 436
Frames from G. Alexandrov's film
Volga-Volga. 1936.

433, 434
Alexandr Deineka. Sketches of
costumes for V. Maiakovsky's play
Bath. 1931.

The village bureaucrat — director
of the club, bookkeeper, accounts
clerk — already wore the coat;
here it was matched with an
overshirt or a peasant shirt with a
side collar requiring no tie, and
trousers tucked into boots. The
official's chief attribute was a
briefcase, and his most reliable
protection was a female secretary

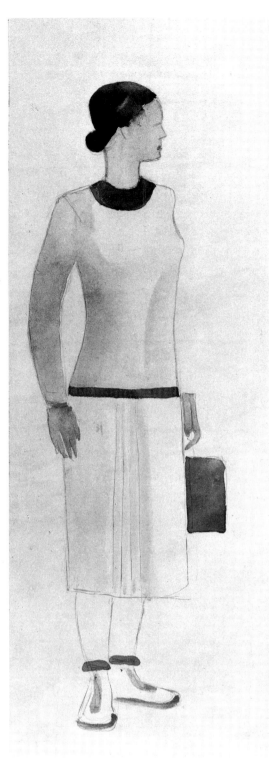

who could pronounce the important word NO. We see such a bureaucrat in the film *Volga-Volga* among a large group of amateur actors who are trying to obtain his permission for a performance. (The director of the club was brilliantly played by Igor Ilinsky.) Nivinsky designed the clothes of Donets coal field employees and of the German workers who had arrived in the USSR to help in the mines. The engineers' wives are accompanied by a maidservant clothed in a modest dress with a white apron, which no longer shocks anyone in the proletarian state. In the Moscow house built for government officals from a design by the architect Iofan, some apartments contain a small room for a servant.

435
436
437

through the phase of initial searches. The development of a style is a long process . . . it cannot be forced. The urgent task of the garment industry is to raise the level of artistic culture. Our duty is to cultivate good taste in the masses."[102]

As is clear from the quotation, in the second half of the 1930s the discussion of fashion continued to pivot on the state of the garment industry and the general cultural level, which remained very low. No administrative measures were taken to change the situation — both industry and artists held on to their former positions.

The issue was aptly formulated by M. Mertsalova: "Before creating fashion, it is necessary to learn to create a costume."[103] It was this phase that was begun by the artists of the 1930s. Experience had shown that the elaboration of a new style was impossible without having mastered the principles of dress design. The attempts to produce a distinctive Soviet fashion by designing clothes with folk motifs could not solve the problem, for it failed to consider costume as an evolving industrial design.

Critics of the 1930s did not deny that valuable experience had been gained in the art of Soviet costume in the past years; this was demonstrated in particular by the new comfortable and functional clothes, which

102.
E. Eikhengolts, "Khudozhest-vennye sovety v shveinoi promyshlennosti" in *Shveinaia promyshlennost,* 1931, no. 9, p. 6.

103.
M. Mertsalova, "Sovremennyi zapadnoevropeiski kostium i ego otrazhenie u nas" in *Shveinaia promyshlennost,* 1934, no. 10, p. 31.

438
439
440

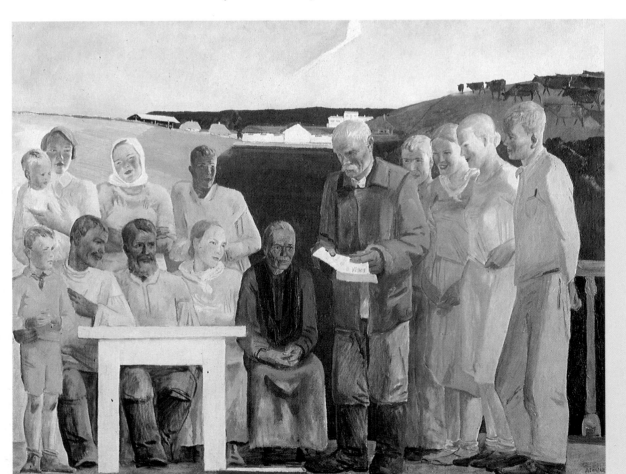

438
Alexandr Deineka. *Collective Farm Team.* 1934.
439
Ignatii Nivinsky. Sketch of costumes for I. Mikitenko's play *A Matter of Honor.* 1931.
440
Frame from G. Alexandrov's film *Volga-Volga.* 1936. Collective farmers in Soviet Russia do not resemble the peasants of prerevolutionary Russia. Young people appear sportsmanlike: they wear knitted football jerseys, ample skirts and trousers, low shoes. Few men have the peasant's customary moustaches and beard. Women go bareheaded, and their rural clothes are almost indistinguishable from urban. The actresses of the village company wear dresses fitted at the waist, narrow skirts with pleats and wool jackets cut like men's coats.

441
N. Anzimirova. Sketch of a
costume for a *Blue Blouse*
performance. 1930.

442-444
Alexandr Deineka. Sketches of
costumes for V. Maiakovsky's play
Bath. 1930.

445-447
N. Anzimirova. Sketches of
costumes for a *Blue Blouse*
performance. 1930.

441 444

442
443

445

446

447

448
Frame for G. Alexandrov's film
Merry Fellows. 1934.

449-451
Frames from G. Alexandrov's film
The Circus. 1936.

The austere years of proletarian
asceticism had ended. The
baroque splendor of 1930s film
stars' attires fired the imagination
of young filmgoers. From Moscow
to the countryside, Liubov Orlova's
admirers emulated, with the help
of their grandmothers' sewing
machines, the actress's distinctive
style.

448
449
450

met the people's requirements for work and everyday life. Without calling this type of costume "design" (a term that did not yet exist), they nonetheless championed it, calling upon artists to seek beauty in simplicity of form.

Throughout the decade, the influence of Western fashion grew on Soviet costume, with critics often deriding its social foundations. "Fashion erects class partitions between social sections and denotes the propertied classes' domination of the poor," wrote the art historian M. Alpatov.[104] Although basically correct, this idea was nevertheless a distillation of the oversimplified views of those years, fixing on only one aspect of the complex phenomenon of fashion and exaggerating it. A broader view was held by V. Shekhman, a garment technology specialist and critic who had worked for many years in garment manufacture. He thought that another problem loomed much larger — that of associating fashion with the economy and technical progress. When studying foreign

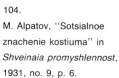

104.
M. Alpatov, "Sotsialnoe znachenie kostiuma" in *Shveinaia promyshlennost*, 1931, no. 9, p. 6.

451

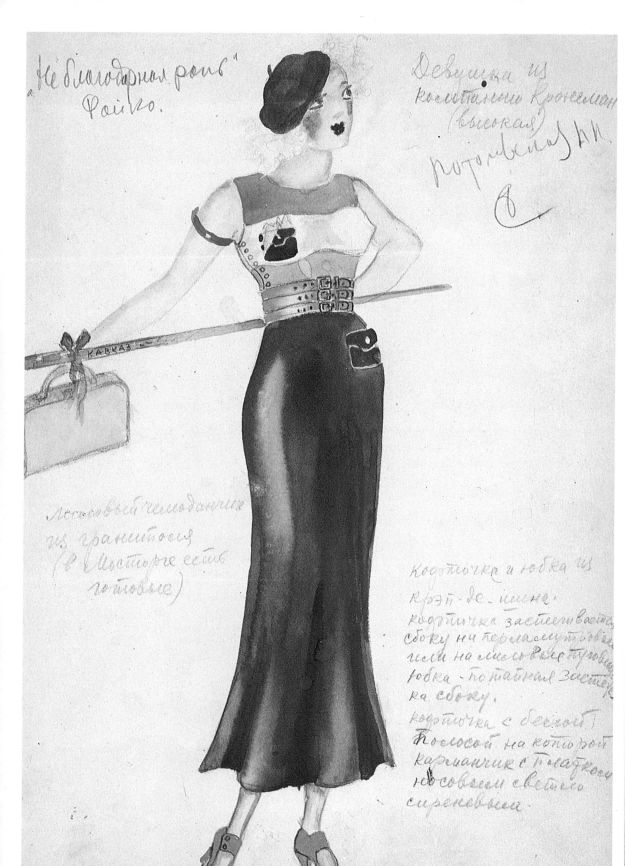

452
Valentina Khodasevich. Sketch of
a costume for A. Faiko's play *A
Thankless Role*. 1932.

453
Frame from G. Alexandrov's film
Merry Fellows. 1934.

454, 455
N. Anzimirova. Sketches of
costumes for a *Blue Blouse*
performance. 1928-31.

454

453

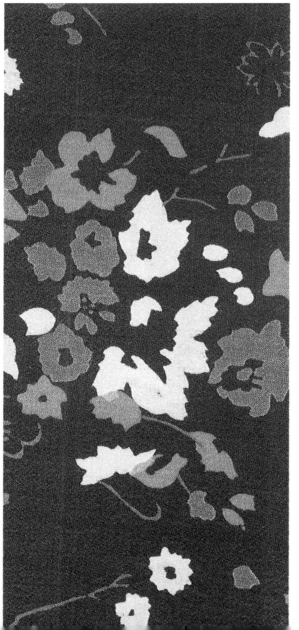

456

M. Nazarevskaia. *Red Army Men Taking Part in Cotton Picking*, cotton print. Early 1930s.

457, 458

Anonymous designer. Silk fabrics with plant motif. 1934-1935.

459

S. Agaian. *Primulas*, silk. Mid-1930s.

460

Frame from V. Batalov's film *The Womenfolk*. 1940. In the mid-1930s, the constructivists' geometric designs and poster fabrics featuring airplanes and construction and harvesting scenes were replaced with plant motifs. The incentive was the 1933 government decision on "inappropriate designs." The idea of florescence and fertility, blessed from the top of the official pyramid, was also reflected in architecture and in the decorative and applied arts. Vases were shaped like baskets of fruit, and fabrics were made in splendid colors. This woman worker from a small collective farm near the Volga, in a 1940 film, wears a sarafan with a traditional floral design.

457
458

experience, he noticed the two-way connection between fashion and the economy, and how seriously fashion could influence the economy. Shekhman, however, did not raise the question of how this important factor could affect the work of Soviet designers.

The House of Clothing Design and the garment factories made an attempt to adopt foreign methods as a harmonized whole, i.e., to learn the principles of tailoring, not just the copying of fashionable models. The ever more frequent demands by the end of the 1930s to develop a Soviet style of clothing that had nothing in common with the style of the West, grew from a national program of combating "the external pernicious influence of the West" and the alleged attempts of "class enemies" to undermine the foundations of Soviet life. In the Stalinist years, cunning fabrications about espionage conspiracies and infiltration by enemies of the people served to disguise the brutal reprisals carried out within the country. Fashion, like all forms of culture, suffered the reverberations of politics.

459   460

461

463

462

461

F. Antonov. *Peonies*, cotton print. Mid-1930s.

462, 463

Anonymous designer. Cotton prints with plant motifs. Mid-1930s.

464

Frame from T. Lukashevich's film *The Foundling*. 1940. The traditional floral motifs in textile design received a new interpretation in the mid-1930s. In this dynamic epoch flowers swirled across the fabric, and stylized flowers made in the wash technique, without an outline, danced and spun. Designs were also executed in the more traditional technique of picot and line drawing, as in a blue-and-golden calico by an anonymous designer. Floral patterns were still popular in the countryside and in the cities. The married couple we see in the frame from the film who think they have come across a homeless little girl, are clothed unpretentiously. The man wears an embroidered shirt and a linen suit, the woman a gaily colored two-piece dress. The hat is the only purely urban element of her outfit.

By the end of the decade, however, it was no longer possible to reject or ignore the European trend in fashion: with the rise of mass industrial production and the cultural level of the people, fashion began to break through national barriers, become international, and dictate its own laws. The new fashion of the late 1930s clearly showed signs of ''militarization,'' with emphasis on a sharp, angular silhouette, exaggerated shoulders, and stiff rhythms in the folds of the skirt. The accessories of military clothes — epaulettes, gold braid, aiglets — began to be used as decorative elements. This confirms the swift reaction of clothing design to global developments and the spirit of the times as expressed in political, social, and cultural life. Like a sensitive barometer, fashion sooner than anything else detected and eventually reflected the growing militarism of the era. The close of the 1930s was a time of a saturnalia of fascism in Germany and Italy, battles over fascism in Spain, and the gradual drawing of Czechoslovakia and Austria into the Second World War.

464

465

466

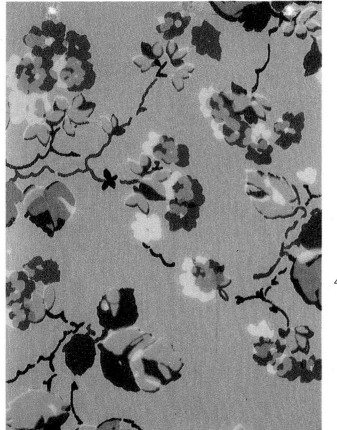

467

465-467

Anonymous designer. Silk fabrics with plant motif. Late 1930s.

468

Kuzma Petrov-Vodkin. *New Home in the Workers' Petrograd*. 1937.

469

Arkadii Plastov. *A Collective-Farm Holiday*. 1937. In the gloomy years of Stalin's repressions, officially approved paintings feature primarily festivities and celebrations. Even the bitter "housing redistribution" of the 1920s is depicted by Petrov-Vodkin as a festive occasion. The aristocrat deprived of part of his apartment peacefully talks with the old peasant. In Plastov's picture we see a collective farmers' feast. Over the tables laden with victuals hangs the cynical Stallinist slogan: "Life has become better, life has become happier!" Fabrics of the period display apple tree blossoms and stalks of rye.

468

469

The process of Soviet clothing design in the late 1930s and the early 1940s was a reflection of developments in the other fields of art, particularly in architecture. Architectural innovation was spurred by the competition for the best design of the Palace of Soviets, a majestic building to be created "in a special Soviet style." The results of the competition were significant not only for Soviet architecture but for Soviet art as a whole. The choice of an individual architectural structure as a historic monument to symbolize the greatness of one person prompted a corresponding architectural style — pseudoclassicism, with its showy splendor, magnificence, and lavish cost.

These characteristics also fully applied to the decorative and applied arts of the time: the interior of public buildings, porcelain, glass, ceramics . . . and, of course, fashion. Particular attention in the latter was paid not to the plasticity of volume (the designing of the form) but to the "façade" of the dress, with a detailed trimming of all elements constituting a peculiar graphic planar drawing.

470

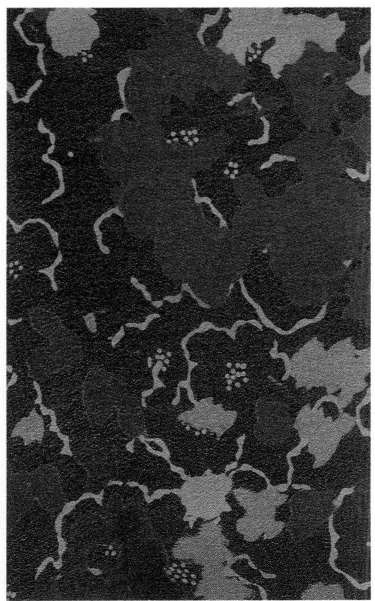

Indicative of this trend was the work of artists at the Scientific Research Institute of Industrial Art (NIIKhP). They created labor-intensive garment designs decorated with folk-style embroidery executed by craftsmen in small artels of the Russian Federation and released in limited numbers onto the domestic and foreign market. In terms of construction, the Institute artists followed the general European fashion trend: their sketches represented dresses rather close-fitted at the waist, of elongated proportions, accessorized by little hats and handbags. These models, however, sported a simple, even oversimplified cut: as a rule, the dresses had a flared skirt, usually with an inverted pleat in front. The designers

471

470

Silk fabric with a plant motif. Late 1930s.

471

Piotr Konchalovsky. *Portrait of Vsevolod Meierkhold*. 1937.

472

Solomon Nikritin. *Self-Portrait*. 1934. The portrait of the theater producer Vsevolod Meierkhold (painted by Konchalovsky, the last portrait before his arrest and death), and Nikritin's self-portrait are more than portraits of talented personalities. These are the images of a hypocritical epoch: the epoch of lawlessness, massacres, and terror.

472

473

474

475

476

473

Mariia Ender. *Experiment in a New Spatial Measure*. 1920.

474

Yurii Pimenov. *The New Moscow*. 1937.

475, 476

Anonymous designer. Silk fabrics with plant motif. Late 1930s. The floral ornamentation of the 1930s was executed in a mild, painterly manner. Textile designers obviously drew from painters' earlier achievements. The industry had at last launched the production of real silks, but not for everyone, of course. The Stalinist elite dwelled amid expensive cars and beautifully flowered silks.

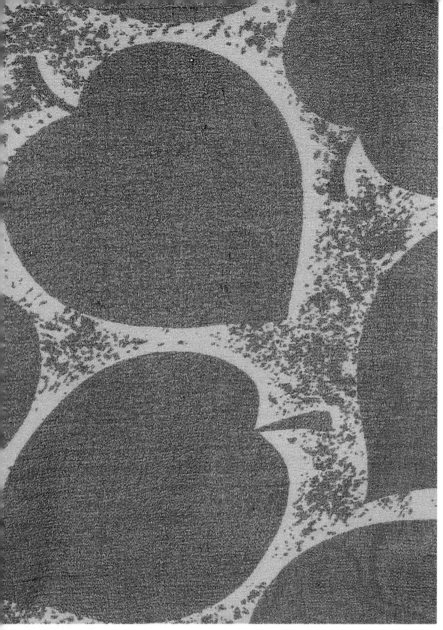

477, 478
Anonymous designer. Silk fabrics with plant motif. Late 1930s.

479-482
Ivanovo textile mill. Second half of 1930s. Archival photographs show the design shop and the sample room in one of the textile mills in Ivanovo. After numerous attempts in the mid-1930s to centralize design production, designers and colorists returned to the factories. These mounted samples were intended for exhibitions, which in the 1930s were held with increasing frequency. The walls display the slogan ''Make every effort to produce beautiful artistic textiles!'' and ''Make Soviet textiles the best in the world!''

478

created quite an assortment of garments: dresses, sarafans, ensembles consisting of a sarafan and a long jacket, blouses, vests, and bathing suits. Every item was sumptuously decorated with hand embroidery, its motifs usually drawn from traditional designs and techniques of Russian ethnic groups: the Mari, Karelians, Chuvashes, and from republics like the Ukraine and Byelorussia. There existed certain canons on the placement of decoration, which followed the constructive peculiarities of the designs, accenting them with narrow patterned bands and ornamental planes on the sleeves and bodice.

The leading NIIKhP designers included Savkova, Ilinskaia, Sapozhnikova, Pench, Zaitseva, and Baronova. Their work displayed an extensive knowledge of contemporary fashions and the principles of folk art. Since handwork was so labor-intensive, their garments were intended for a narrow circle of wearers.

An especially interesting designer of this group, and the one who best

480

481

482

483

484

485

483-485

Elena Savkova. Sketch of an ensemble including blouse, sarafan, and jacket with short sleeves. 1939.

486, 487

Elena Savkova. Sketch of an ensemble including a dress with bare shoulders and a jacket with long sleeves. 1939.

486

487

488

Anonymous designer. Sketch of an embroidered inset for a dress. 1939. A cult of Russian folk art sanctioned by the authorities arose in the late 1930s. Folk art museums were opened, folk song and dance ensembles were formed; even architects used folk motifs. Although in the 1920s people renounced their past, in the decade that followed they turned back to their roots. This tendency was felt in clothes as well. The Scientific Research Institute of Art Industry, created to revive the ''Russian style,'' made designs for embroiderers and lacemakers for small quantities of richly ornamented dresses and costumes in silk and linen.

488

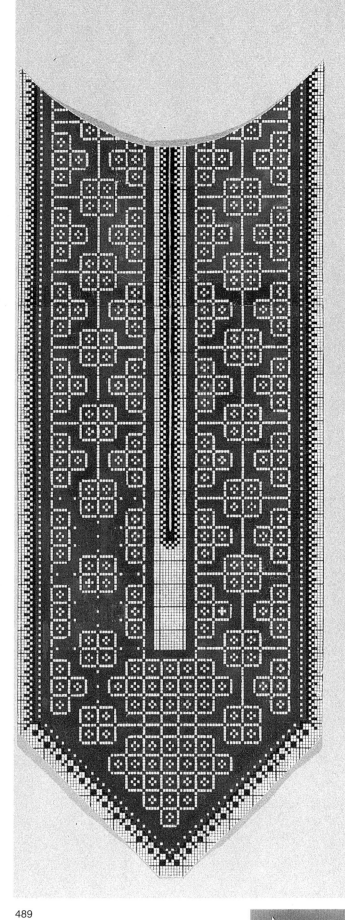

489

491

492

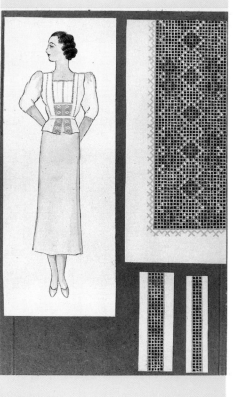

490

489
Elena Savkova. Sketch of a dress decorated with embroidery and appliqué. 1939.

490
Anonymous designer. Sketch of a dress. 1939.

491
Elena Savkova. Sketch of a dress. 1939.

492
Elena Savkova. Sketch of a costume. 1937.

expressed the style of the epoch, was Elena Savkova. In 1939, one of the artist's typically elegant designs was shown at the International Exhibition in New York. It was very simple in construction: a straight dress with puffed sleeves. Its distinction, however, consisted in a skillful and rich ornamentation covering the bodice, and the red-patterned embroidery lining the upper parts of the sleeves and the hem. Use was also made of a special type of embroidery — *krestetskaia* — and the so-called "Vologda bugles" with gold thread. The dress was made of georgette crêpe, and the embroidery in "moulinet" and gold thread. Savkova designed three equally rich versions of this dress. Her individual style is easy to recognize in a white ensemble with a red belt, consisting of a sarafan and a long jacket (the trim of the sarafan combined embroidery and lace), in a model of a white dress with embroidery in red thread covering the entire bodice, and an elegant white-and-blue ensemble of a dress and a jacket.

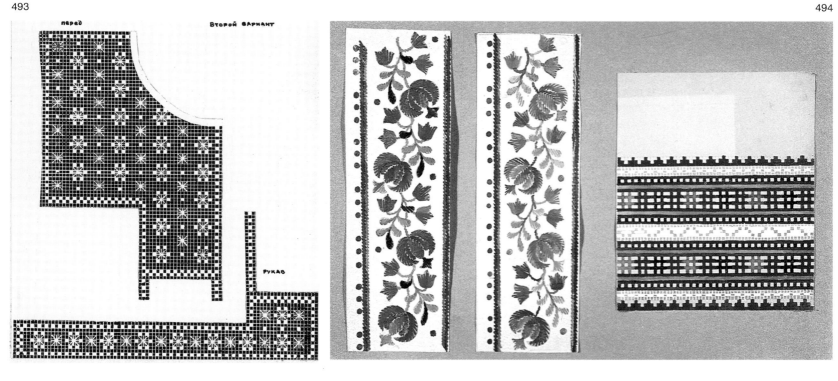

493, 494

Anonymous designer. Sketches of embroidered insets for dresses. 1939. The cut of these dresses and costumes generally followed European style — fitted at the waist and of elongated proportions. They were one-of-a-kind pieces characterized by a wealth of decoration, including lace insets and embroidered details, and were very successful at international exhibitions. Savkova's work was awarded a prize at the 1939 New York exhibition.

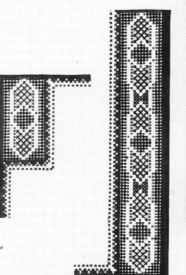

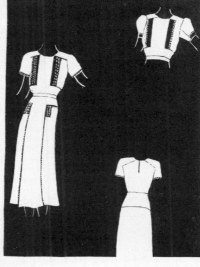

495

496

495

Nina Aizenberg. Sketch of a costume for A. Korneichuk's play *Platon Krehet*. 1936.

496

Anonymous designer. Sketch of a dress ornamented with embroidery. Versions of ornaments. 1939.

497, 498

K. Bozhneva, M. Vysheslavtseva. Sketches of a children's coat and a woman's blouse of knitted fabric. 1938-1939. In the mass-produced clothes of the late 1930s, use was made of the folk costume of the people of the Caucasus and the Russian North, and of the military uniform.

497

498

1939

Божиева и Вышеславцева. 1939

Although the creation of handmade masterpieces did not constitute a phenomenon of great importance in the history of Soviet costume, it did mirror the current interest in creating a new national style with traditional motifs. Nonetheless, however gifted the NIIKhP masters might be, the fruits of their efforts would always ring slightly false: a truly folk art is created by the people themselves, as it was in prerevolutionary Russia.

In 1939, Leningrad hosted a review of industrially produced clothing in which some of the republics participated for the first time. Work to create fashionable garments had by then begun in Uzbekistan, the Ukraine, and Transcaucasia. The review showed that the general level of textile products had improved a great deal since the early 1930s, but mass production of clothing has still not taken hold. In June 1941, on the eve of World War II, the first group of designers graduated from the Moscow Textile Institute. Their work was to make itself felt after the war.

499

499
Viktor Koretsky. *If War Breaks Out Tomorrow*, poster. 1938.

500

500

Alexandr Lakticnov. *Tank Trainees*.
1938.

501

Performance by the song and dance
ensemble of the Moscow military
district. 1938. In 1938 the rattle of the
approaching war was heard on all
sides. Koretsky's poster displays the
words from a popular song "If war
breaks out tomorrow...," and shows
the country in arms. The cheerful
soldiers in Laktionov's painting,
working peacefully on a bulletin
board, are there to convince the
viewer that the country's borders are
well guarded. The dashing military
dance with sabres recalls the
cavalry's triumphs in the civil war and
promises victories to come.

501

502

504

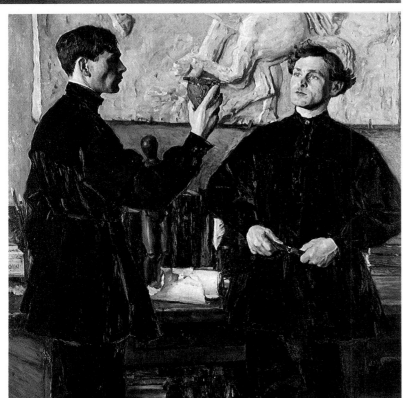

503

505

502

Vasilii Yakovlev. *Portrait of Mikhail Mlimov*. 1936.

503

Mikhail Nesterov. *Portrait of the Artists, the Korin Brothers*. 1930.

504

Georgii Riazhsky. *A Letter*. 1939.

505

Mikhail Nesterov. *Portrait of the Sculptor Vera Mukhina*. 1940.

506

Mikhail Nesterov. *Portrait of the Artist Elizaveta Kruglikova*. 1938. The garments that actors, artists, and sculptors wore represented their creative profession. Creativity in Russia had always been associated with romantic costume — for example, velvet blouses and coats teamed with a silk ruffle.

506

РОДИНА-МАТЬ ЗОВЕТ!

ВОЕННАЯ ПРИСЯГА

507

507

A team of actors after their performance for the Leningrad Front soldiers. 1943.

508

508

Soviet pilots after their return from an air mission. 1943.

509

Frame from M. Zharov's film *The Troublesome Business*. 1946.

510

Air Force officers' wives, after being evacuated to the rear, attend politcal education classes. Lugansk. 1943.

Garment production suffered colossal damage during the war. The textile and garment factories in the occupied territories either ceased to exist or were evacuated to the rear. The garment industry served only the needs of the army. An actress could come to the front line in a silk dress, fanciful hat and soldier's canvas boots. An evacuated pilot's wife wore high-heeled shoes and a luxurious silver fox both to the factory and to her political education club.

509

510

511

Iraklii Toidze. *The Motherland Summons You!* Poster. 1941.

512, 513

Soldiers of the Western Front between battles. 1945.

511

Clothing During World War II (1941-1945)

World War II caused tremendous damage to every facet of Soviet life, including the clothing industry. The garment factories that happened to be on occupied territory either ceased to exist or were evacuated to the rear. From the beginning of the war the garment industry was completely reoriented to serve the army.

Any progress in textile and garment production technology during the war was out of the question — innovation took place mostly in the development of films and coatings for army equipment, and also in leather substitutes. In the war years considerable changes took place in the military uniform: more modern and practical fabrics began to be used, while the introduction of officers' ranks led to the modification of the insignia system. Despite the immense difficulties in the country's economy, the garment factories managed to provide the army with the necessary clothes.

The most widespread types of civilian clothing were the comfortable quilted jackets made of simple and cheap gray cotton that were worn everywhere, both at work and at home, because of the cold. They can probably be called the most popular uniform of the war years. Military

514

515

514

Vasilii Yakovlev. *Portrait of General Panfilov*. 1942.

515

Soviet soldiers carrying their Guards' banner. 1943. During the war the Soviet Army uniform underwent many changes. Military ranks, abolished under an egalitarian impulse after the 1917 Revolution, were reintroduced, and with them the insignia. The cut of the greatcoat was altered, the *budenovka* headpiece was replaced by the warm fur cap with earflaps in winter, and the peaked or field cap in summer. The sheepskin that General Panifilov, the hero of the Battle of Moscow, wears was the Soviet soldiers' salvation during the four winters of the war. As they joked in the army, ''the sheepskin helped win the war.''

516

Vladimir Lebedev. *Portrait of Artist Lebedeva*. 1943.

517

Vladimir Lebedev. *Portrait of a Girl Student*. 1940. It was in these feminine clothes that the women — wives, mothers, sisters, and daughters — were remembered by the soldiers of the Soviet army in the trenches of Stalingrad and Kingisepp.

516

517

greatcoats and tarpaulin boots were also quite common. Shopping bags were replaced everywhere by gas-mask bags.

Much of the population, however, were wearing what remained of pre-war civilian clothes, and the cheerless gray and dark tones predominated in the street. By 1943, manufacture of printed fabrics and ready-made clothing began, mostly at the evacuated factories and in Moscow. The shortage of textiles and of ready-for-service garments, however, was felt for a long time, and their assortment left much to be desired.

The wartime hardships made people intensely frugal with their wardrobes, and they wore severe everyday dresses and suits that in Europe were called "utility dress." Of a simple cut, unassuming, without trimming or decorative elements, this rather anonymous outfit could be, if not fashionable, at least serviceable for several years thanks to its "neutrality."

This mode of dress became very common in postwar years, particularly for business and everyday wear. It proved stable and long-lasting. Life was austere, and therefore the simplest and most modest clothes were the most appreciated.

520

518
Muscovites meet demobilized soldiers on the platform of the Rzhevsk railway station. 1945.

519
Topographers in the streets of destroyed Stalingrad, 1944.

520
Vladimir Vasiliev. *The Demobilized*. 1949. It was with relief and joy that women traded their soldier's blouses for their first postwar dresses.

Publications

Report of Narkomtorgprom (People's Commissariat of Trade and Industry) on the Organization of a Central Institute of Garment Industry

January-February 1919

Prior to the October Revolution, clothing manufacture in Russia was limited mainly to handicraft enterprises. Big factories producing goods in quantity were rare, and were set up mostly for the manufacture of military service uniforms. Dress styles were determined by trends in foreign fashion, which was adapted to the customs and tastes of bourgeois society and in most cases did not meet the basic requirements of beauty, hygiene and comfort.

The socialist reorganization of industry necessitates the elimination of the small handicraft workshops and the creation of large factories with the best possible technical, sanitary, and hygienic equipment requiring the least expenditure of labor, and which do away with unhealthy production conditions while producing new forms of clothing characterized by hygiene, comfort, beauty, and elegance.

The concentration of production in big factory-type enterprises now taking place in the garment industry makes new demands on the personnel's theoretical and practical knowledge, as well as the scientific and technical organization of enterprises, and makes the training of managers especially urgent.

The complete absence of textbooks and essential materials in all branches of training in the garment industry sets another task: to systematize all the existing materials concerning the organization of manufacture and to create textbooks and manuals; to find the best methods of organization of production and instruction, and, finally, to create a central scientific and educational institution to unify and co-ordinate the work of the separate institutions in this field.

The Central Institute of the Garment Industry is to be such an institution, with two main tasks to perform: first, to examine and solve, on the basis of scientific research and practical experimentation, all problems of scientific organization of production and of work and to decide on the hygienic and artistic types of clothing, and the methods of instruction at the vocational educational establishments; second, to train technical organizers and production managers, and also teaching staff competent in their specific field, for vocational training.

In accordance with the main tasks, the Institute's curriculum is to include scientific and technical, artistic, graphic, and economic subjects, as well as hands-on learning in workshops. The course of studies of four to six semesters is to consist of practical training and upgrading in the chosen specialty, the study of scientific disciplines closely associated either with the technology or the economics of production, and also the study of artistic subjects that can improve the production process, both from the point of view of technological development and the beauty and elegance of the goods.

The drafting of a detailed curriculum is entrusted to the Council of the Institute; because of the importance of the broadly interpreted and properly arranged practical work in the given specialty, it should be assigned 50 percent of the study hours. Correlation between the principal groups of subjects — artistic (drawing, sculpture, the history of arts as related to the history of artistic forms in production, etc.), scientific and technical (science of machines, manufacturing processes, etc.), and economic (design of factories, calculations, industrial accounting, etc.) — is organized for the Institute's departments depending on their specific tasks.

The group of subjects common to all departments include: social science, the history of culture, the history of production, hygiene, drawing, and the history of the arts.

The Institute's future students need enough experience and general education to acquaint themselves thoroughly. The Institute must have laboratories, a special library, a museum, and a permanent exhibition reflecting the work of the Institute and its establishments. The immediate task of the Institute is to arrange during the summer of the current year courses for the officials of specialized schools. The courses shall also be attended by professionals sent by various organizations and institutions in different localities, both from educational establishments and mills, in agreement with the All-Russian Union of Workers of the Garment Industry.

The Institute is to combine and co-ordinate the activities of the Garment Industry Union, the bodies regulating production, and the institutions in charge of vocational training.

The plan for the organization of the Institute envisages using the existing instruction courses of the vocational second section of the Moscow Department of Public Education and, as auxiliary institutions, the first special needlework and tailoring workshops, the first industrial-art costume workshops under the Chief Committee for Vocational Training, and the production workshops and courses under the Garment Industry Union.

In order to expedite the organization of the institute, it is necessary to concentrate in one building the above-mentioned training establishments and workshops, which will make it possible to associate the personnel of these institutions for joint regular work with the training establishments and workshops used as laboratories for practical work and experiments. During the transfer of these institutions, the Institute should revise their staff, program, and methods of instruction according to the Institute's Statute, both regarding the teaching personnel and students, and scientific and instructional activities.

In view of the growing crisis in vocational training owing to the shortage of the required teaching personnel, training aids, and literature, etc., the organization of the Institute is an extremely urgent task.

MOAORS, f. 967, op. 1, d. 88, l. 4. (Copy.)

Statute of the Central Institute of the Garment Industry

January-February 1919

I. General Principles

1. The Central Institute of the Garment Industry is a higher scientific and educational institution having as its aim:

a) to deal with, on the basis of scientific research and practical experiments, all scientific problems connected with the production of clothing and included in the curricula of vocational educational establishments (schools, courses, etc.), such as providing materials on the history of the garment industry and the industrial geography of Russia and other countries, introducing hygienic and artistic forms of clothing, developing scientific methods of industrial engineering and organization of manufacturing enterprises of the garment industry, etc.;

b) to develop methods of instruction and of dissemination of scientific and practical knowledge in the field of vocational training;

c) to prepare instructors and managers of different qualification levels both for educational establishments and for the organization and management of production.

2. The Central Institute of the Garment Industry is founded under the Chief Committee for Vocational Training, and its scientific and educational work is conducted with the direct participation of the All-Russian Union of Workers of the Garment Industry and the respective organs regulating manufacturing activities.

3. The Institute enjoys the rights of a juridical individual and has a seal with its appellation.

II. Scientific and Educational Activities

4. The scientific plan is drafted by the Council of the Institute in accordance with the general tasks in the field of vocational education and industrial engineering and is subject to approval by the Chief Committee for Vocational Training.

5. All scientific work of the Institute is to be based on research and practical experiments, and necessitates extensive employment of vocational education officials and instructors and the technical personnel of garment industry enterprises, both on a full-time basis and through competitions for various kinds of practical work.

6. The curriculum is drafted by the Council of the Institute on the basis of obligatory use of the laboratory method of instruction and is subject to approval by the Chief Committee for Vocational Training. The scope of the subjects to be taught and their distribution throughout the semesters and years of study, as well as the forms of practical work in industry, are decided by the Council of the Institute.

7. The term for preparing instructors and managers is to last from four to six semesters, whereas the course for those with practical experience and corresponding theoretical knowledge may be reduced to two semesters, depending on the degree of their training.

8. On the decision of the Council of the Institute and on respective approval, there can be opened occasional short-term courses in different specialties of the garment industry.

9. To carry on scientific research and also to ensure the best system of instruction, the Institute will have a number of auxiliary institutions, namely: special libraries, museums, exhibitions, laboratories, factory art and industrial art workshops, and other instructional auxiliary facilities.

III. Students

10. The Institute admits as its students persons of both sexes not younger than 16 years of age, preference being given to those delegated by the All-Russian Union of Workers of the Garment Industry and to persons who have previous experience in vocational training.

11. Students are specially provided for on general terms.

12. Those who have completed the course in all required subjects, have done practical work and passed all the prescribed tests, acquire the rank of instructor, organizer or manager. Students who have passed separate stages receive a certificate thereof.

IV. Instructors

13. The post of instructor can be filled by a person who has received an appropriate education and has practical experience in his specialty. The procedure of choosing the teaching staff is established on general terms.

Note: Instructors are persons who give lectures or independently direct the students' work.

V. Administration

14. The Administration of the Central Institute is based on general terms with the indispensable condition that the Council of the Institute includes representatives of the Central Committee of the All-Russian Union of Workers of the Garment Industry, of the bodies regulating production: Chief Garment Board, Chief Furs Board and the bodies of the People's Commissariat of Public Education.

MOAORS, f. 967, op. 1, d. 88, l. 5. (Copy.)

Regulations of the Sokolniki Soviet Educational Industrial Art Studios of Costume in Moscow

23 January 1919

1. The Sokolniki Soviet Educational Industrial Art Studios of Costume in Moscow have as their object to prepare aesthetically

and technologically competent specialists in the field of costume manufacture.

2. For the attainment of the above object, the Studios will:

a) establish permanent contact with local industry and with individual organizations and model workshops, museums of industrial and applied arts, fine arts societies, professional unions of respective enterprises and workshops, state art studios, etc., with the purpose of exchanging aids and collections, inviting lecturers and instructors, etc.;

b) have the required equipment in each specialty;

c) found an applied arts and technical library, a collection of applied art specimens in the Studios' specialty, arrange lectures and demonstrations of technical information, etc., evening and Sunday courses for persons wishing to study special subjects, and exhibitions of productions of those working at the studios;

d) provide to the instructors opportunity for periodical trips both within the republic and abroad for work in their specialty, in accordance with the decision of the Council of the Studios.

3. The Studios give instruction in: fancy needlework, sewing, tailoring, etc.

4. The learning of a specialty at the Studios is accompanied by courses in:

a) fine arts (drawing, painting, sculpture);

b) art history (fine arts and applied arts);

c) the study of style and costume;

d) the history of production and its significance in the national economic system;

e) the theory of design, tailoring and drawing;

f) accounting;

g) the science of materials;

h) occupational hygiene and labor legislation;

and any other subjects required to develop the creative abilities of those training in the workshops, in accordance with the resolution of the Council of the Studios.

Note 1. The content of the course is determined by the curricula drawn up by the education and art commission and after their consideration by the Council of the Studios as presented to the Education Department.

Note 2. The curriculum is to have considerable flexibility, so that it is adaptable to special assignments, and so that some subjects can be introduced for separate groups working at the studios.

5. The normal duration of the course shall be three years divided into semesters. Depending on the degree of preparation for work in the Studios, the length of the course may be changed by the Council of the Studios.

6. Access to the Studios is open to all those who wish to learn the given specialty, to receive advanced training or to discover the latest production processes; the education of this category of student does not follow definite curricula and terms, but the required theoretical instruction may be achieved through lectures and discussions.

7. Admission to the Studios is for persons of both sexes not younger than 16 years of age.

8. Those who have completed the course at the Studios receive certificates to that effect.

9. The Studios are under the authority of the People's Commissariat of Trade and Industry, within the Education Department, to which they present in due time both the account of their activities and detailed expenditure estimates to be treated in accordance with the established procedure.

10. A Council of the Studios is set up to co-ordinate the Studios' activities with the industry and to keep in touch with the economic life of the region, and also to exercise general management. The Council shall include: the entire personnel of the Studios; representatives of the students (one from each group); representatives of the People's Commissariat of Trade and Industry, the Public Education Department of the Sokolniki Soviet of Workers' Deputies, and the Sokolniki National Economy Department, one from each; and representatives of the Trade Unions (trades related to the Studios), and Fine Arts Societies, one from each.

11. The Council of the Studios considers:

a) curricula drafted by the educational art commission and program of separate courses compiled by the groups of directing specialists;

b) annual estimates and accounts of the education and administrative-economic activities in the Studios;

c) all matters of a general nature concerning the Studios' activities.

12. In their educational and art activities the Studios are administered by the Educational-Art Commission, which includes all artist-masters heading individual studios and which is entrusted with:

a) all affairs of the Studios' routine work, the division of students into groups, assignment of the work of instruction in individual courses and other teaching jobs to the members of the Instructors' Board, etc.;

b) organizing all work of the Studios along the lines of their general plan, and carrying out the decisions of the Council of the Studios;

c) making up by specified dates estimates and accounts concerning the studios' educational activities and submitting them to the Council of the Studios and the Education Department of the People's Commissariat of Trade and Industry, and also to the Public Education Department of the Sokolniki Soviet of Workers' Deputies.

13. For business management of the Studios, the Council elects a managing Commission, which includes one representative from each group of those working at the Studios. The Commission has the following functions:

a) to see that the equipment of the Studios is kept in good repair and safe; to expend, with the permission of the Council of the Studios, the financial resources;

b) to draw up in due time estimates and accounts and to submit them to the Council of the Studios, to the Education Department of the People's Commissariat of Trade and Industry, and to the Public Education Department of the Sokolniki Soviet of Workers' Deputies.

14. To solve problems of an educational nature, to work out curricula, etc., there may be organized commissions having as their members all those who are employed as instructors at the Studios.

15. All instructors for the Studios are chosen by the Council from among those who are known by their work in the given specialty or by their educational activities.

Note: To provide the necessary personnel for the Studios, all vacancies for instructors and managers are brought to the notice of the Education Department and public art organizations.

16. Management of each individual studio is entrusted to a specialist, a costume artist selected by the Council of the Studios for a term of five years.

17. The means for maintaining the Studios are made up of:

a) the funds allocated for their maintenance from the Treasury;

b) donations from public organizations;

c) receipts from the sale of goods produced by the Studios

and other money incomes.

Note: The procedure for the expenditure of the Studios' funds is determined by the regulations worked out by the Managing Commission and approved by the Education Department of the People's Commissariat of Trade and Industry.

18. The Studios are granted all the rights with the named individual and are entitled to:

a) have a seal of a prescribed standard with the name of the Studios;

b) collect fees;

c) arrange exhibitions of the Studios' works;

d) take orders that are in line with the educational objectives of the Studios.

MOAORS, f. 967, op. 1, d. 88, l. 1-2.

(Attested copy.)

Information on Competitions for the Best Interior of Workers' Living Quarters

29 January 1919

The Professional Trade Union of Artists has decided to hold five competitions, one of which is for architects, two for painters and two for sculptors. Architects, members of the Union, are invited to make a design of a workers' house for four families. Painters will participate in competitions for the best interior design of the rooms and decoration of the workers' house, and also for the best sketches of suits, dresses, etc.

Sculptors are to compete in the design of the best tea set and silverware case.

The two best works in each competition will be awarded prizes. The best designs in the architectural competition will be awarded prizes of 1,200 rubles each. The winners in the last two competitions will receive prizes of 500 rubles each.

The jury includes sculptor Blokh, artist Brodsky, artist Khodasevich, and architect Dubinetsky.

The money for the competition has been provided to the Professional Trade Union of Artists by the cultural and educational department of the Petrograd Council of Trade Unions.

The newspaper *Zhizn iskusstva*, 23 January 1919, p. 3.

Information on the Creation of New Work Clothes

The first conference was held at the headquarters of the Commissariat of Public Health to discuss the creation of new work clothes which would meet present-day requirements. Invited to the conference were artists, physicians, industrial engineers, and others. The persons who have made it their aim to create a new work dress believe that the present work dress — the work blouse — is not rational enough. The great Russian revolution ought to exert its influence not only on the internal man but on the external one as well. The new clothes must not only be comfortable and elegant but they must also fully meet current economic conditions and hygienic requirements.

The newspaper *Zhizn iskusstva*, 21 May 1919, p. 1.

Minutes of a Meeting of the Industrial Art Commission of the State Academy of Artistic Sciences (GAKhN)

23 March 1922

The meeting was attended by: Comrades S. A. Kotliarovsky, N. P. Lamanova, D. I. Ivanov, A. V. Filippov, and Davydova.

N. P. Lamanova made a report on "The Use of Generally Accessible Fabrics for Costume" and showed samples made after artists' sketches under her supervision.

Present-day conditions of production demand generally accessible fabrics for clothes and accessories. The artistic aspect of the product depends upon the creative initiative and imagination of the artist, who outlines the basic shape of the garment. The design proceeds from the fabric. Industrial art can be pursued only in the context of model workshop laboratories and the participation of artists.

After hearing the report by N. P. Lamanova and examining the samples made by a group of artists, who used such plain and available fabrics as hopsacking, the Commission pointed out the necessity of co-ordinating the work of the artists, and provided them with the opportunity of using a model workshop or laboratory set up for this purpose.

The Commission is of the opinion that such workshops can considerably improve the results of the manufacture of garments for large sections of the population and that expenses thereon (especially for the supply of the necessary fabrics) will be well repaid, not only culturally and artistically but economically as well.

TsGALI SSSR, f. 941, op. 7, d. 2, l. 9.

(Original.)

Conclusion

Made by I. Averintsev, Chief of the Institutions of the Fine Arts Section, the People's Commissariat of Public Education of the RSFSR, after the inspection of the work of the Commission of Art Industry of the State Academy of Artistic Sciences.

March 1922

The work of the Commission of Art Industry indicates that it does not fully represent specialists working in different branches of art industry but has as its members a mere two or three theorists and two occasional productionists, in consequence of which all theoretical premises and conclusions of the Commission are one-sided and amateurish, which is extremely harmful in such a dynamic realm as art industry. An authoritative Commission is needed, including members of the Union of Applied Art Workers.

TsGALI SSSR, f. 941, op. 7, d. 2, l. 14.
(Original.)

Application of the Society of Textile Artists to the Decorative Art Section of the State Academy of Artistic Sciences for assistance arranging the First Exhibition of Soviet Textiles in Everyday Life.

December 1927

The Society of Textile Artists, which has as its members artists and colorists working in the factory and handicraft industries and whose main objective is to improve the aesthetic qualities of textiles, arranges the first exhibition of Soviet Textiles in Everyday Life.

The purpose of the exhibition is to attract the attention of the public to the serious and decisive role of the artists and colorists employed in the manufacture of everyday fabrics. Such an exhibition is being held for the first time, therefore it must reflect the work that has been done in textile production during the past decade, and also reveal the importance of textile artists.

The present-day situation in textile production certainly is difficult: designers and artists are scattered, disorganized, and lack the impulse for the healthy creative competitions that are found in all other fields of art (printing, porcelain, etc.). The exhibition is expected to inspire a broad-based unification of artists and to promote their creative initiative.

The Society of Textile Artists believes that such an important field of artistic culture cannot remain unnoticed by the Academy of Artistic Sciences, which is the center of artistic life and which includes all branches of art.

Therefore the Society expects that the Academy of Artistic Sciences will give it the necessary and competent support in arranging the exhibition Soviet Textiles in Everyday Life and in the Society's further efforts, which include research assignments (for instance, the history of development of cotton printing, the study of aesthetics, ethnicity, etc.).

The Society of Textile Artists was created in the spring of 1927

on the initiative of young artists who were graduating from the textile department at VKhUTEMAS and immediately received a lively response among artists and colorists working in the biggest textile factories. The Society's board included the artists F. V. Antonov, chief of the art section of Ivtextil (Ivanovo Textiles); L. V. Maiakovskaia, chief of the spray-painting shop at the Trekhgornaia Textile Mill; F. S. Roginskaia, art critic; P. P. Rusin, chief of the design section of the former Tsindel Factory; N. N. Sobolev, handicrafts researcher, the author of the book *Cotton Print in Russia*; and colorist A. K. Auer, technical manager of the Hübner textile mill. The Society has been sanctioned by the Art Department of the Central Administrative Board of Science.

TsGALI SSSR, f. 941, op. 7, d. 30, l. 11.
(Original.)

Reference

Nadezhda Petrovna Lamanova has made theater costumes for the Art Theater since the early years of its existence *(In Dreams, The Cherry Orchard*, and others).

At the present time N. P. Lamanova is a member of the Theater's staff as a costume consultant, and all costumes for plays either being produced (*The Dead Souls*) or being prepared for production (*Talents and Admirers, Molière*, and others), are made under her direct guidance and with her personal participation. This long cooperation with N. P. Lamanova, which has produced such splendid results, has given me grounds to consider her an indispensable, talented and rare specialist in the theory and practical manufacture of theater costume.

Director of the Moscow Academic Art Theater named after Gorky,
K. Stanislavsky

Seal of the Moscow
Art Academic Theater
Certified copy
MKhAT

N. P. Lamanova
Project of Organization of the Studio of Elegant Work Clothes

1919

The objective and tasks of the Studio are:

a) To introduce elements of art into the manufacture of clothing;

b) To adapt contemporary costume to the life and needs of the Soviet Republic today;

c) To prepare costume artists for teaching at vocational schools, and for working in the garment industry and in theater;

d) To form instructors who will train highly qualified personnel for the industry.

The program of the Studio comprises all sectors directly concerning contemporary costume and related auxiliary disciplines.

The principal course, based on a combination of the theory and practice of costume, falls into two parts:

I. The construction of costume:

  a) Its shaping, and the human figure as its object;

  b) The conception of a figure as a volume and a silhouette;

  c) The construction of costume based on geometric forms;

  d) Material and its connection with the form and purpose;

  e) Color;

  f) Decoration;

  g) The purpose of costume.

II. The Manufacture of costume:

  a) Sketching a costume;

  b) Combining fabrics texturally;

  c) Seam techniques;

  d) Execution of decoration and various types;

  e) Tailoring.

Auxiliary disciplines:

  a) Anatomy and proportions;

  b) Hygiene;

  c) The history of civilian and theatre costume;

  d) Folk costume, its history and techniques;

  e) Methods to make simplicity a characteristic feature of workers' garments, in contrast to the garments of the bourgeoisie;

  f) The dynamics of contemporary costume;

  g) The utilitarian nature of contemporary costume; its purpose as work or everyday clothes, holiday attire, sportswear, professional dress, outer clothing, and headgear.

The work would be incomplete, however, if it is confined only to the production section. Since the project involves more than a mere workshop or school, but the development of an "image," it is also necessary to create a theoretical section which is to be artistic, cultural, and educational. It will be directed toward an artistic comprehension of everyday life, and of costume (both past and present) in particular. Lasting benefits could accrue from instruction in simplicity, harmony, and expediency. It is only by turning to the history of the arts that one can understand the artistic requirements of the epoch and the hidden forces that influence them.

The ideological framework is erected in a deliberate and gradual way: through courses, seminars, exhibitions, etc. The Studio's work is to be conducted according to an artistic and marketable plan. Everything produced at the Studio's workshops will be put on sale, and the purchases will confirm that the chosen methods are correct and that the undertaking itself is viable.

N. P. Lamanova
The Russian Style

An interesting endeavor in the field of contemporary costume is the modification of the forms and character of folk costume and their application to everyday Soviet life. The rationality of folk costume, thanks to our ancestors, can serve as the ideological

and plastic forms for our urban clothes. The basic forms of folk costume are always wise. Thus, taking for example the folk costume of the Kiev province, we shall see that it consists of an outer jacket, a skirt (*plakhta*) and a chemise with embroidered sleeves and hem. This folk costume consists of work clothes intended for manual labor, and is easily transformed from winter into summer wear and from daily into holiday with simple additions such as beads, garlands, and a bright-colored apron. From this common costume, so in tune with everyday living and working conditions, and based on a sense of the physical characteristics of the Russian figure, it is easy for us to create urban garments. By accepting the wonderful color of traditional costumes and distributing it rhythmically on a rationally made costume, we create the kind of clothes that are in harmony with our contemporary life.

Karasnaia niva, 1923, no. 30, p. 32.

N. P. Lamanova
On Contemporary Costume

Our present Russian generation can no longer tolerate the tyranny of fashion and ignorance concerning costume. Here, as everywhere else, we want to understand the meaning and process of manufacture. Even in folk costumes, despite their dependence on tradition, we see their inherent rationality — the purpose for which the dress was made. We see work, everyday, and holiday garments; outer garments, in their turn, are divided into elegant and plain. The same principle of classification of costume according to its purpose is found in complex contemporary urban life as well, where the many and varied occupations dictate that a person's work clothes must be rational — though comfortable and simple, they must be in keeping, above all, with the worker's specific occupation (tight-fitting clothes, for instance, cannot be worn by those whose work requires movement). On the contrary, holiday attire, with the observance of the same simplicity and comfort, can be more individualized to the wearer, with more complicated forms and richer colors. The city has its festivities and entertainments, therefore the holiday costume is also divided into morning and evening dress; the latter can even be adapted into a costume for the stage, requiring, of course, more decoration and a more accentuated form.

Thus, when working on a costume, one should clearly see its ultimate purpose, and this should tell you the best choice of form, color and fabric.

The peculiarities of the fabric itself should always be born in mind, for the fabric does not yield to coercion — if you try to go against its nature, the results will always be bad. When all its characteristics are kept in mind, a fabric, even the cheapest, can serve as the starting point for a beautiful form, just as a definitely conceived form requires its own definite fabric.

But even more important is to take into consideration the individual for whom the costume is made; its uniqueness and the consequent tailoring required to achieve the most harmonious silhouette. Here we come to the very core of a contemporary conception of costume, in contrast to the outmoded fashionable approach.

Traditional fashion is a great equalizer: it disregards the peculiarities and defects of the individual figure (recall the crinolines and fashionable tight-fitting ''swaddling'' skirts). But every person, despite any physical shortcomings, natural or acquired, has the right to appear harmonious. The present-day conception of costume attempts to do this by deliberately altering the human figure for the sake of more pleasing proportions, through a creative construction of costume.

It was for some time an ingrained prejudice that a corpulent figure was best dealt with by compressing it into a corset and narrow clothes; in fact this emphasized even more its disproportion.

A corpulent figure should be approached from quite a different direction: in this case the silhouette can be lightened only by concealing its disproportion through its being crossed by planes of another form. And, vice versa, with a thin woman's figure, it is necessary at the same time to be careful not to deprive it of its very lightness, lightness not in an aesthetic sense but in the sense of mobility, of movement. Our epoch rejects everything static in life and in art. It is for the purpose of enhancing dynamism and also for decorative effect, that a costume should be based on the principle of contrast. A costume, therefore, may be both narrow and wide. This love of contrast in clothes is found in folk costume as well; in the Ukrainian *plakhta* (skirt), for example, which was narrow around the hips and, in contrast, had a bell-shaped corselet. Many silhouettes in fashion magazines of the past year provide extremely poor examples of this concept, showing a lack of any understanding of contrast in the figure and an utterly static effect. One example was narrow armholes and narrow sleeves in a narrow dress. This absence of contrast and, consequently, of dynamics makes the figure dry, monotonous, and lifeless. Quite opposite is the effect of a kimono dress: the wide upper parts of the sleeves combined with the narrow lower part of the dress produce a light, contrasting and vivid silhouette. Thus, before being tailored, the costume must be constructed. To construct a costume well, the figure must be mentally divided into geometric shapes to invoke a clearer image of its true shape. In projecting the figure onto the plane, and drawing it, we must regard it as a number of planes. If, owing to the defects of the figure, these planes are disproportionate, by dividing these planes by other planes of different shapes (for instance, by intersecting them with triangles or rectangles), we can achieve a more harmonious correlation of parts and thereby a more constructed silhouette.

In contemporary costume divisions can be used to conceal a long waist, to make a short figure look taller or a tall figure look shorter (by dividing it in two).

Each component of the dress represents a part of the total geometric figure. We cannot, therefore, regard the sleeves and the collar as separate elements. The neckline (round, triangular, square, high, or low), must be in harmony with the dress and, vice versa, the shape of the dress must harmonize with the neckline or collar. Two principles apply here: construction in contrast to the form or in strict conformity with it. The same must be said concerning the decorative aspect of the dress. Like the collar and sleeves, the finishing of the dress with embroidery, leather, or fur must not clash with the general form.

The finishing of a garment with one color or another is important for its entire construction: it can intensify the rhythm of the planes, enhance the form itself, lighten it or weigh it down, depending on the color.

The growing interest in the artistic and constructive aspect of costume today is quite symptomatic. If through this interest and these experiments — which are made, in part, by the scientific laboratory of the clothes workshop under the People's Commissariat of Public Education — we achieve comfortable, harmonious, and useful costumes, we shall thereby enrich our everyday life and, at the same time, do away with the prejudice and hypocrisy which have so far made working women copy bourgeois fashions instead of developing their own creative principles in clothes. The new costume will be in line with the new life: working, dynamic, and aware.

Krasnaia niva, 1924, no. 27, pp. 662-663.

N. P. Lamanova
On the Rationality of Costume

Costume is one of the most sensitive manifestations of social life and psychology.

The unprecedented categorical restructuring of the entire social organism and the birth of the new mass consumer in Soviet Russia inevitably bring in their wake an equally sharp change of costume. Hence the necessity of creating a new costume that combines the artistic sense of form peculiar to our epoch with the purely practical requirements of our time.

In contrast to West European fashion, whose changes depend on commercial considerations, we must assume as a basis of our costume considerations of social hygiene, the requirements of work, etc. It is not enough to create merely a comfortable costume; we need to ensure a proper correlation between the artistic elements of costume and the new forms and aspirations of the emerging new life. All these conditions require methods of artistic construction and practical realization of contemporary costume in the interests of mass production.

Costume is in a sense a continuation of the body. It has functions to perform, like our bodies, in life and in work, and this is why clothes must be rational — they must not hinder the wearer, but in fact help him. Hence the most important factors dictating clothes design are the following:

1) The wearer's personal mood and taste in one form or another (the wearer's style).

2) The style of the epoch; its cultural physiognomy.

3) The form of the individual expressed in a definite silhouette.

4) The fabric, which, being in itself a given form, predetermines some of the elements of the shape we are creating.

5) The utilitarian purpose of the costume.

Thus, the task of creating an artistic costume involves the integration of the figure, the fabric and the purpose into a common form as appealing as possible in the eyes of the epoch and the wearer. The above can be expressed in the practical formula:

For whom

From what

For what purpose

and all this is synthesized in *how* (the form).

In creating the form according to these principles, it is necessary to observe its strict subordination to the plastic laws of proportions and relationships which govern any art. Such an interpretation of costume not only reflects the purely external life of society but also impels one to scrutinize the domestic, psychological, historical, and national features of the Russian people; this, naturally, will lead to research into folk art, as manifested in the handicraft industry. Here will be found ample opportunity to use the splendor of folk art motifs and their profound rationality so in keeping with the Soviet way of life. Traditional embroidery, laces, and linen fabrics are combined with the contemporary sense of form brought into existence by the renewed social and psychological life of society.

Manuscript. Archives of T. Strizhenova.

Theses of the report of V. F. Stepanova at the Institute of Artistic Culture on the status and tasks of a constructivist artist in the textile print industry in connection with the work at the First Textile Print Factory

5 January 1924

1. The status of an artist in the textile print industry. The factory obtains designs for printing through:

   a) a design section at the factory itself;

   b) an artistic atelier of samples outside the manufacturing enterprise.

2. The design section is isolated from the production and managerial bodies of the factory.

3. The artistic ateliers are also cut off from production.

4. Problems of relations with the consumer, pandering to tastes and fashion.

5. The experience of the First Textile Print Factory in improving relations between artists and producers. Combating primitivism in the work of an artist. Attempt to link the artist with production. Changing the old-fashioned approach to the consumer. Serving the mass consumer.

6. The tasks of a constructivist artist working in the textile print industry. The transfer of production work from the studio to the factory. Gradual reorganization of the "design section" into a creative unit.

7. Working both with the production managers of the factory and the chemical laboratory. Participation in seasonal projects.

8. Establishing contacts with fashion magazines and fashionable dressmaking and tailoring establishments.

9. Advertising the products of the textile print industry in the press and campaigning for a rational costume. Refining the consumer's tastes. Enlisting his services in the drive for rational fabrics and costume.

10. Eradication of the deep-rooted view of the ideal of artistic design as imitation of painting. Eliminating organic design in favor of geometrized shapes.

TsGAOR SSSR, f. 5721, op. 1, d. 2, l. 5.

Printed in Italy
in September 1991
by ARBE Industrie Grafiche - Modena